COOKING FOR TWO
—— WITH YOUR ——

AIR FRYER

ONE CONVENIENT APPLIANCE, **75** PERFECTLY PORTIONED RECIPES

BY **DREW MARESCO** AND THE EDITORS OF

Best Recipes .co

COOKING FOR TWO

WITH YOUR

AIR FRYER

ONE CONVENIENT APPLIANCE, **75** PERFECTLY PORTIONED RECIPES

BY **DREW MARESCO** AND THE EDITORS OF

Best Recipes.co

Best.Recipes.co

Published in the United States by
Best Recipes Media Group, LLC

www.bestrecipes.co

ISBN: Print 978-0-9987812-5-9

eBook 978-0-9987812-6-6

Printed in China

Cover and Book Design by Drew Maresco

Photography by Drew Maresco and Dallyn Maresco

10 9 8 7 6 5 4 3 2 1

First Edition

TO ANYONE LOOKING FOR EASY RECIPES CREATED FOR TWO (OR JUST YOU)!

CONTENTS

COOKING FOR TWO WITH YOUR AIR FRYER

INTRODUCTION

It seems like the air fryer became a household staple overnight, and it's really no wonder why. Who doesn't love the idea of making healthier versions of their favorite fried foods? If I'm really honest, once I heard it could revive sad leftover french fries to their original glory, I was sold! Beyond that, though, I wasn't convinced the air fryer could do serious cooking, like roasting chicken or baking a cake, but boy, I was wrong.

I bought my first air fryer from a secondhand store because I just wasn't convinced it could actually be everything it was promised to be, and I wasn't about to waste a bunch of money on one. In the beginning, I wasn't super excited to start using it. It probably doesn't help that I bought it on a whim, and it didn't come with an instruction manual. But once I started using it, I used it more and more often. And I will say, starting off reheating food was probably the best thing I could do because it allowed me to get more comfortable with it.

Excellently-reheated food was all it took, I was hooked on this thing, and I realized its popularity was no fluke. So I began experimenting with recipes, making more foods from scratch, and everything was coming out amazing. Well, almost everything! Sure there's a bit of a learning curve, but it is essentially a super-efficient miniature convection oven. Beyond its obvious benefits, some other things I hadn't considered are how air fryers don't heat up your house too much (which is a godsend in the summer where I live), they're quite easy to clean, and they're pretty compact for what they do. Now that compact size can be a double-edged sword for many. Of course, we don't want something that takes up a lot of space, but the smaller the air fryer, the less food you can cook in it, which isn't super helpful if you have a large family. Luckily, air fryers are coming in larger sizes that will accommodate most families, and they are still not too large. But I realized its average small size was PERFECT for a very specific group of people...

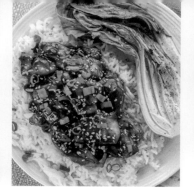

So, who's the air fryer for? Well, everyone! But when I started seeing my friends ask for them on their wedding registries, my parents got one as they became empty-nesters, and even my single friends showing theirs off on Instagram, that's when it really hit me! The small size of the air fryer was perfect for anyone looking to make smaller batches of food! When I lived alone, I would make large batches of food, then get sick of eating the same thing for days, and hopefully remember to freeze the rest. I found myself not wanting to turn on the oven to cook something "just for me," but getting takeout every night gets expensive, and I definitely understand those frustrations. So I started experimenting with homemade food in the air fryer just for myself and was pleasantly surprised by how much food I could actually make in it!

That leads us to this book; I wanted to take the benefit of the air fryer's small size and couple it with recipes designed to make cooking for two (or just one) as easy as possible. No more seemingly endless leftovers or forgotten mystery foods in the fridge. With this book, you get to enjoy perfectly portioned meals (and even desserts!) plus a few tips for air fryer success, and smart shopping tricks! I hope that you'll find this cookbook to be more than just another cookbook for your shelf but a true guide to cooking smaller batches and keeping food waste to a minimum!

Whether you're a seasoned home cook or just starting out, you'll find the recipes in this book are very straightforward and approachable for everyone! And to make sure these recipes taste as great as possible, fresh ingredients are used throughout! If you're like me, once I find those recipes that really resonate with me, I make them again and again. Because they're so straightforward, I encourage you to make them as written, then next time you make them, try adjusting them to your preferences — turning them into your own! That's the best way to become a better cook, and it's definitely encouraged!

DREW MARESCO
Author

TIPS FOR SUCCESS

GETTING FAMILIAR WITH YOUR AIR FRYER

Converting conventional recipes into air fryer recipes isn't too difficult but may require a little trial and error. The rule of thumb is to reduce the temperature by 25° F (15° C) and reduce the cooking time by half, checking/flipping/turning the food about halfway through.

When converting recipes, I recommend making ones you've already cooked before because you already know how it's supposed to turn out. That way, you'll have a great benchmark to compare with versus starting with a new recipe. If a new recipe doesn't turn out, it'll be difficult to pinpoint the cause.

AIR FRYER PRESETS

Many air fryer models have different presets for common foods. While these can be very helpful, many models don't have them, so our recipes don't include using them.

CROWDING

If ever there was a cardinal rule not to break, it's this one! Avoid the temptation of cramming in that extra tater tot; it isn't worth it! All kidding aside, airflow is crucial for that crispy exterior you're looking for, but if you're willing to shake the basket (or stir the food) often, you may get away with having a little more food than what's recommended without too much of an issue.

SHAKE SHAKE SHAKE

As mentioned above, shaking the basket (or stirring on the tray) helps with even cooking and browning. I always recommend flipping, shaking, or rotating food, at least one time, halfway through cooking. But admittedly, I have a tendency to be a bit over-attentive to foods as they cook. I've heard many argue that this step shouldn't be necessary as the air fryer is designed for maximum airflow, and while I can't argue that point, I know I've never regretted flipping my food.

HOT SPOTS

When rotating food, knowing the hot spot of your air fryer will be incredibly helpful. If the back right-hand corner of your air fryer is the hottest, that's the food that needs to get moved to a cooler spot. This prevents uneven cooking, and even burning!

AIR FRYER Q&A

You have questions, and I have answers! Whether you're an air fryer pro or just starting out, the following Q&A has some helpful tips for air fryer success.

DO I NEED TO PREHEAT?

There's much debate on this exact topic, and the answer isn't so simple. I used to tell people that there was no need to preheat their air fryer until I bought a different model... This new one absolutely needed preheating because foods just didn't come out the same if I skipped it. So now, as a general rule, I let the air fryer run for about 5 minutes at the temperature stated in the recipe before putting my food in, just to be safe.

DO I NEED OIL?

While technically, no, you don't "need" to use oil in your air fryer, and I know many people have purchased these so they never have to cook with oil again. But I will say that a little oil goes a long way with the air fryer because it affects the color of your food, adds to the flavor, and affects the texture. So I highly recommend getting an oil sprayer so you can have even, but minimal, oil coverage on your food.

WHAT STYLE IS BEST?

I honestly have not found much difference between air fryer shapes (or styles), but brands do vary. In my experience so far, I do think the oven-style models are a little easier to work with since you can arrange your food on trays. That being said, I've used a basket style for years and have had zero complaints!

WHAT SIZE IS BEST?

It's easy to think the smallest air fryer is best, especially when you're cooking for two, but I am going to challenge that thought for a moment. I recommend buying the largest one you're able to store in your home. The main reason for that, the larger air fryers allow more room for not only your main entree but maybe even your side dish, too. Smaller air fryers hold smaller amounts of food, meaning you'll be cooking in batches, even for small-batch cooking. You can always cook less food in a larger air fryer, but you can't stuff more food into a small one without affecting the taste and texture.

DO I NEED ACCESSORIES?

While you absolutely do not need accessories to succeed with your air fryer, I do recommend getting them if you can. Accessories can make cooking (or even baking) in your air fryer much easier! So if you're willing and able to, get an accessory kit that fits the size of the air fryer you own. Check out a few of our favorite accessories on page 14.

SMARTER SHOPPING FOR TWO

There are generally two frames of mind when grocery shopping for two, avoiding food waste or saving money. That's not to say you can't have the best of both worlds; it can just be tricky. I put a list of tips together to help you achieve either (or both) goals.

MEATS

Head to the nearest local butcher and order exactly what you need. This avoids any leftovers that may get forgotten about. Seeing a bulk package of meat calling your name? Go for it! Buying items like meat in bulk will save you tons of money yearly. To avoid any waste, immediately separate the meats into smaller packages (about 1-2 servings per package) and freeze them. That way, you never thaw too much and will have the exact amount you'll need for the recipes in this book.

VEGETABLES

Vegetables can be a bit tricky, but it's not impossible! Often you'll see vegetables like carrots packed in big bundles, which is way too much for just two people. Steer your eyes towards the organic section because many grocers sell those loose and by the pound. If your grocer has a salad bar, you're in real luck — just grab what you need! Don't be afraid to opt for frozen vegetables either; you can find many vegetables in two serving portions, and frozen at peak season, so you know they'll taste great!

GRAINS AND PASTA

Besides storage space, there are very few negatives to buying these items in bulk. They keep for long periods and are an excellent way to save some money. Just make sure you stock up on items you frequently use because there's no logical reason to stock up on items you seldomly use.

BROTHS AND STOCKS

I have found a handy ingredient that avoids food waste and saves space is soup bases, such as 'Better Than Bouillon.' These bases can come in organic and low-sodium, and are packaged in a small jar with a long shelf life, so you'll always have broth ready to go when you need it. There's little cost difference between the cartons of broth and jars of concentrate. If you're anything like me and you forget about that open carton of broth in the fridge, you'll save money right off the bat. Not to mention you'll get more servings out of a jar of concentrate and the convenience of always having broth on hand.

CANNED GOODS

There's no shame in purchasing convenience items. Some of my personal favorites include marinara sauce, tomatoes (stewed, diced, whole, you name it), beans, and some vegetables. If you do find yourself with any of these leftover, they will keep in the freezer for up to 3 months!

OIL

Avoid low smoke point oils when cooking in the air fryer and aim to use oils like avocado, ghee (clarified butter), canola, or vegetable oil. They have a smoke point that works well with the high heat of the air fryer. For the recipes in this book, I used canola and vegetable oil. Obviously, because of their smoke points, but they're also the most affordable of the above options.

CHEESE

Packaged cheese comes in all shapes and sizes. Unfortunately, like most convenience products, the smaller the packaging, the more expensive it becomes. I don't go through a lot of cheese but can't help wanting the best bang for my buck. I have found that cheese freezes fine for 6-9 months if stored airtight! But it is best to only use it in cooked dishes due to the texture change after it's been frozen.

HERBS AND SPICES

Herbs, both fresh and dried, add so much flavor to your food. We wouldn't have the fantastic meals we know and love without them! And while I do love the flavor of fresh herbs, they can get pretty pricey, and frequently you end up buying way more than you'll need for a recipe. So to save money and avoid food waste, I used dried herbs and spices throughout this book. Beyond savings, some other benefits you'll find to using dried herbs and spices are their concentrated flavors (meaning you'll use less for more flavor), and there's no risk of them burning in your air fryer!

HELPFUL
ACCESSORIES

A. Baking Pan

B. Silicone Oven Mitts

C. Tall Wire Rack

D. Silicone Tongs

E. Short Wire Rack

F. Metal Skewers

G. Perforated Parchment Paper

H. Oven-Safe Ramekins

I. Silicone Hot Pad

J. Baking Dish

K. Aluminum Foil

L. Oil Sprayer

EVO SPRAYER PHOTO BY TONY ALLEN | EVOOILSPRAYERS.COM

SANDWICHES
AND ANYTHING ELSE
SERVED ON BREAD

While sandwiches may not be the first thing that comes to mind to make in your air fryer, the results may just surprise you. From a Croque Monsieur to subs, burgers to grilled cheese, and just about anything else served between bread, this chapter explores several different cooking techniques and cuisines from all around the globe. Enjoy!

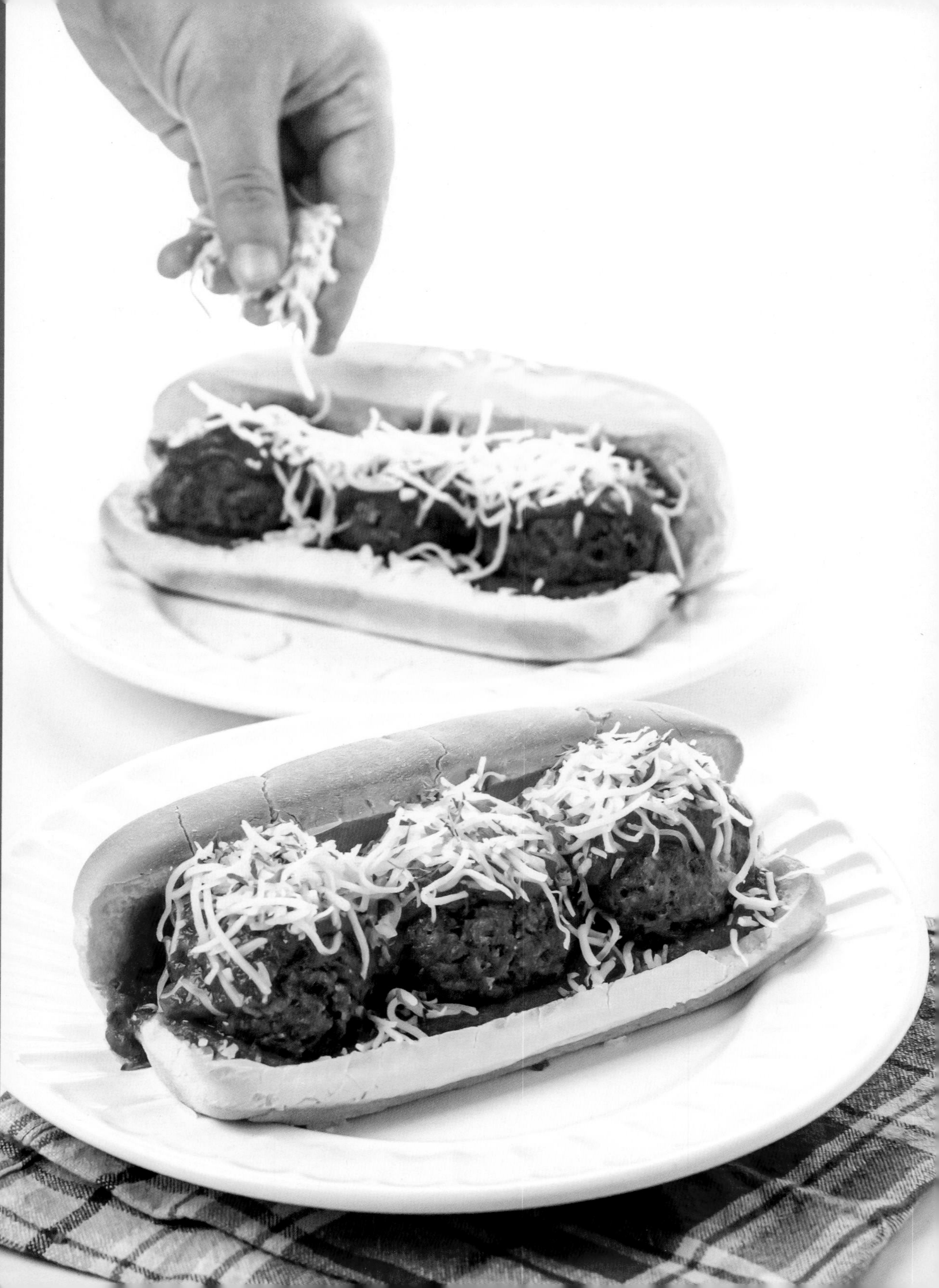

PESTO AND MARINARA MEATBALL SUBS

The air fryer makes some of the best meatballs you'll ever have! They're delicate, yet hold together, and have a slightly crispy exterior. These already great meatballs are only made better by infusing them with pesto and serving them up as a submarine sandwich.

COOK TIME: 12 MIN | EFFORT: EASY

INGREDIENTS

- 8 ounces (227 g) ground beef
- ⅓ cup (82 ml) prepared pesto
- ½ teaspoon salt
- ½ teaspoon onion powder
- ½ teaspoon garlic powder
- 1 egg
- 3 tablespoons (18 g) grated Parmesan cheese
- 2 tablespoons (10 g) Italian seasoned breadcrumbs
- 1 cup (250 ml) marinara sauce, divided
- ¼ cup (28 g) shredded mozzarella, divided
- 2 sub buns
- Oil spray

DIRECTIONS

1. Preheat the air fryer to 350° F (170° C).

2. In a large bowl, using your hands, combine the beef, pesto, salt, onion powder, garlic powder, egg, Parmesan, and breadcrumbs. Then divide and shape into six equally-sized meatballs. Spray the air fryer with oil, add the meatballs, and cook for 6-10 minutes, flip and cook for 2 more minutes. Transfer to a plate, cover, and set aside.

3. Assemble each sub with ½ cup marinara, three meatballs, and 2 tablespoons of mozzarella.

CAJUN CHICKEN CHEESESTEAKS

While I love the classic Philly cheesesteak, I have made room in my heart for this Cajun-inspired version. Hoagie rolls are stuffed with Cajun-seasoned chicken, peppers, and onions. Top it all off with a simple Cajun bechamel sauce and you won't be missing the steak in this sandwich!

COOK TIME: 15 MIN | EFFORT: EASY

INGREDIENTS

- 8 ounces (227 g) chicken thighs, cut into bite-sized pieces
- ½ teaspoon salt
- ¼ teaspoon pepper
- ¼ teaspoon chili powder
- ¼ teaspoon Cajun seasoning
- 1 small red pepper, diced
- 1 small onion, diced
- 2 hoagie rolls
- 4 slices provolone cheese
- Oil spray

SAUCE

- 2 tablespoons (28 g) butter
- 2 tablespoons (16 g) flour
- 1 cup (240 ml) milk
- 2 teaspoons (11 g) Dijon mustard
- ¼ teaspoon salt
- ¼ teaspoon pepper
- 1 teaspoon Cajun seasoning

DIRECTIONS

1. In a small bowl, toss together the chicken, salt, pepper, chili powder, and Cajun seasoning until fully coated.

2. Preheat the air fryer to 350° F (170° C). Spray the air fryer with oil, add the chicken, peppers, and onions, spray with oil, and cook for 10-14 minutes, stirring and spraying again halfway through.

3. Meanwhile, in a small saucepan over medium heat, melt the butter. Whisk in the flour, stirring continuously for 2 minutes. Gradually add in the milk, stirring after each addition. Add in the mustard, salt, pepper, and Cajun seasoning, stirring until combined. Set aside.

4. Place two slices of cheese per hoagie roll. Add the chicken and vegetables and top with the sauce.

MEDITERRANEAN BEEF PITAS WITH ROASTED VEGETABLES

The unique flavors of Mediterranean food are often made from spices you likely already have in your pantry. Nutmeg, allspice, paprika, and garlic powder transform a simple cut of beef into an extraordinary meal. Paired with roasted vegetables (also made in the air fryer) and creamy hummus, this sandwich will bring the flavors of Mediterranean skewers right to your own kitchen.

COOK TIME: 15 MIN | EFFORT: EASY

INGREDIENTS

- 8 ounces (227 g) beef roast, cut into bite-sized pieces
- ¼ teaspoon nutmeg
- ¼ teaspoon allspice
- ¼ teaspoon paprika
- 1 teaspoon garlic powder
- ½ teaspoon salt
- ¼ teaspoon pepper
- 1 small zucchini, sliced into half-moons
- 1 small red pepper, thinly sliced
- 1 small red onion, thinly sliced
- ¼ cup (59 ml) hummus
- 1 pocket pita
  Oil spray

DIRECTIONS

1. Preheat the air fryer to 400° F (200° C).

2. In a large bowl, add the beef, nutmeg, allspice, paprika, garlic powder, salt, and pepper; tossing to coat. Spray the air fryer with oil, add the beef, zucchini, peppers, and onions, spray with oil, and cook for 10-14 minutes, stirring halfway through.

3. Slice the pita in half, open the pockets and fill each with 2 tablespoons of hummus and half of the beef and vegetables.

SAUSAGE, PEPPER, AND ONION HOAGIES

Sausage, peppers, and onions are a classic combination and one that you'll see a few times in this book. In its first appearance, you have this trio slathered in a tomato-based sauce and loaded into a hoagie roll! All I can say is 'Yes, please!' Trust me, your mouth will thank you!

COOK TIME: 25 MIN | EFFORT: EASY

INGREDIENTS

- 1   small onion, thinly sliced
- 1   medium green pepper, thinly sliced
- ½   teaspoon Italian seasoning
- ¼   teaspoon salt
- ¼   teaspoon pepper
- 8   ounces (227 g) sweet Italian sausage links
- 2   garlic cloves, minced
- ¼   cup (59 ml) white wine
- ¼   cup (59 ml) water
- 1   tablespoon (11 g) tomato paste
- 4   slices provolone cheese
- 2   hoagie rolls, toasted
-      Oil spray

DIRECTIONS

1. Preheat the air fryer to 360° F (180° C). Add the onions, peppers, Italian seasoning, salt, pepper, and sausage to the air fryer. Spray with oil and cook for 16-20 minutes, stirring halfway through.

2. In a medium saucepan over medium heat, add the roasted peppers and onions, garlic, white wine, water, and tomato paste. Slice the sausages diagonally and add to the pan. Cook for about 4-5 minutes, until the mixture thickens slightly. On each hoagie roll, place a slice of cheese and half of the sausage mixture.

STEAKHOUSE BBQ BACON CHEESEBURGER

If you love a grilled burger but feel like bringing out the grill just to make two is a bit overkill, I hear you! These air-fried steakhouse burgers will challenge the ones you get from your favorite restaurant. When you see a burger topped with crisp bacon, fried onions, cheese, and bbq sauce, you know it's going to be good.

COOK TIME: 12 MIN | EFFORT: EASY

INGREDIENTS

- 8 ounces (227 g) ground beef
- ½ teaspoon Worcestershire sauce
- ½ teaspoon paprika
- ½ teaspoon pepper
- ½ teaspoon salt
- 1 teaspoon brown sugar
- ¼ teaspoon garlic powder
- ¼ teaspoon onion powder
- ⅛ teaspoon ground cumin
- 2 slices cheddar cheese
- 4 bacon strips, cooked
- 2 tablespoons crispy fried onions
- 2 tablespoons (30 ml) BBQ sauce
- 2 brioche burger buns
  Oil spray

DIRECTIONS

1. Preheat the air fryer to 400º F (200º C).

2. In a small bowl, using your hands, combine the ground beef, Worcestershire sauce, paprika, pepper, salt, brown sugar, garlic powder, onion powder, and cumin. Divide the mixture into two patties. Spray the air fryer with oil and add the patties, cooking for 8-12 minutes, flipping halfway through.

3. Assemble the burgers on the buns with the BBQ sauce, cheese, bacon, and crispy onions.

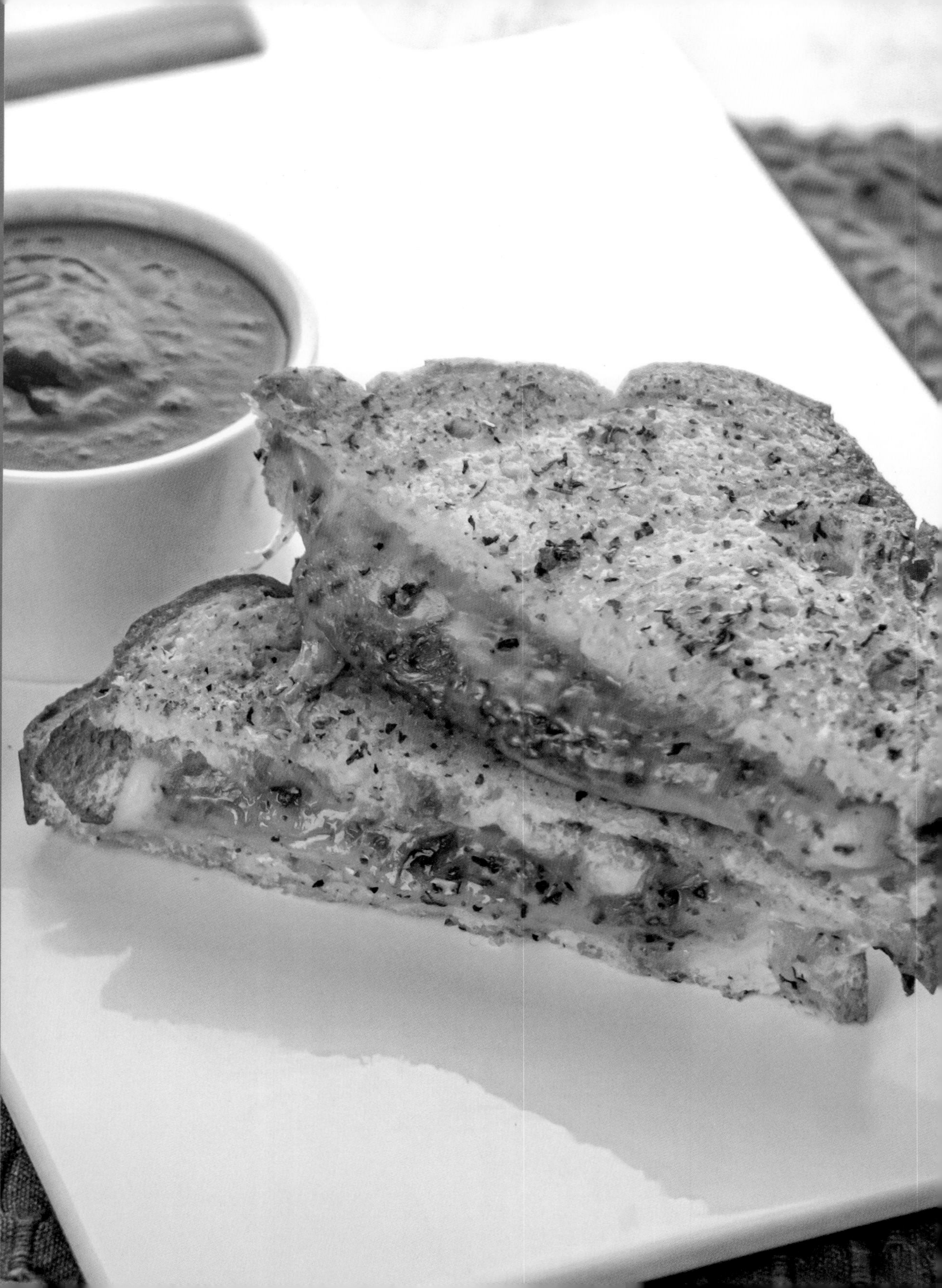

ITALIAN-STYLE GRILLED CHEESE

What's more nostalgic than a classic grilled cheese sandwich? I often crave them but I also like to have a little fun with them by changing up the cheeses and flavors. In this version, provolone and mozzarella melt into this deliciously-cheesy, pesto-infused, served-on-garlic-bread grilled cheese! Is it a bit over the top? Sure. Is it worth it? You betcha!

COOK TIME: 8 MIN | EFFORT: EASY

INGREDIENTS

- 4 slices sandwich bread
- 2 tablespoons (28 g) butter, divided
- ¼ teaspoon garlic powder
- ¼ teaspoon Italian seasoning
- 4 slices mozzarella
- 4 slices provolone
- ¼ cup (59 ml) pesto, divided
- ¼ cup (59 ml) marinara sauce, divided

DIRECTIONS

1. Preheat the air fryer to 380º F (190º C).

2. Butter one side of each slice of bread and season with garlic powder and Italian seasoning. Assemble the sandwiches, butter side down, two slices of provolone, pesto, and two slices of mozzarella. Top with the last bread slice and secure with a toothpick. Place in the air fryer and cook for 4-8 minutes, or until browned, carefully flipping halfway through.

3. Serve with marinara on the side for dipping.

CROQUE MONSIEUR

What do you get when you slather a ham sandwich with a Dijon bechamel sauce and gruyere cheese? This sandwich! If you've never heard of it before, it may sound odd but it's a classic French sandwich and it's incredible! Also, if you serve it with a fried egg on top you have a Croque Madame!

COOK TIME: 15 MIN | EFFORT: MODERATE

SAUCE

- 2 tablespoons (28 g) butter
- 2 tablespoons (16 g) flour
- 1 cup (240 ml) milk
- 2 teaspoons (11 g) Dijon mustard
- ¼ teaspoon salt
- ¼ teaspoon pepper
- Pinch nutmeg

INGREDIENTS

- 2 tablespoons (28 g) butter
- 4 slices brioche bread
- 12 slices ham
- ½ cup (121 g) shredded Gruyere cheese, divided

DIRECTIONS

1. In a small saucepan over medium heat, melt the butter. Whisk in the flour, stirring continuously for 2 minutes. Gradually add in the milk, stirring after each addition. Add the mustard, salt, pepper, and nutmeg, stirring until combined. Set aside.

2. Preheat the air fryer to 400º F (200º C).

3. Butter one side of each slice of bread. Layer the sandwiches butter side down, six slices of ham, 2 tablespoons of bechamel, and 2 tablespoons of gruyere. Top with a slice of bread, and secure with a toothpick. Place in the air fryer and cook for 3-5 minutes, or until the bread is slightly browned, flipping halfway through.

4. Carefully top each sandwich with 2 more tablespoons of bechamel and 2 more tablespoons of gruyere. Return to the air fryer and cook for 3-5 minutes, or until the cheese is bubbling and browned in some areas. Slice and serve.

CARAMELIZED ONION PATTY MELTS

A patty melt may be best described as a cross between a grilled cheese and a cheeseburger. Perfectly seasoned beef burgers are paired with caramelized onions and served on toasted bread with melty swiss cheese. Try this fun-textured sandwich the next time you're in the mood for a good burger!

COOK TIME: 40 MIN | EFFORT: MODERATE

INGREDIENTS

- 4 tablespoons (56 g) butter, plus more if needed
- 1 small onion, diced
- 8 ounces (227 g) ground beef
- ½ teaspoon Worcestershire sauce
- ½ teaspoon paprika
- ½ teaspoon pepper
- ½ teaspoon salt
- 1 teaspoon brown sugar
- ¼ teaspoon garlic powder
- ¼ teaspoon onion powder
- ⅛ teaspoon ground cumin
- 4 slices sandwich bread
- 4 slices swiss cheese
- 1 tablespoon (14 g) mayo
  Oil spray

DIRECTIONS

1. In a medium skillet over medium-high heat, melt 1 tablespoon of butter. Add the onions and cook for 20 minutes, stirring often, until desired color is reached.

2. Preheat the air fryer to 400º F (200º C).

3. Meanwhile, in a small bowl, using your hands, combine the ground beef, Worcestershire sauce, paprika, pepper, salt, brown sugar, garlic powder, onion powder, and cumin. Divide the mixture into two even patties. Spray the air fryer with oil, add the patties, and cook for 5-9 minutes, flipping halfway through.

4. Butter one side of each slice of bread. Assemble the sandwiches, butter side down, one slice of swiss, burger, half of the onions, another slice of swiss, and mayo. Top with a bread slice, and secure with a toothpick. Place in the air fryer and cook for 4-8 minutes, or until browned, flipping halfway through.

BANG BANG SHRIMP PO' BOYS

This famous appetizer gets served up sandwich-style! Panko-breaded shrimp are tossed into this famously spicy, yet creamy, sauce then served on a hoagie roll, topped with lettuce and tomato. I'm not lying when I say, making this into a sandwich is my favorite way to eat this shrimp!

COOK TIME: 12 MIN | EFFORT: EASY

SAUCE

- ¼ cup (56 g) mayo
- 2 tablespoons (30 ml) sweet chili sauce
- 2 teaspoons (10 ml) Sriracha

INGREDIENTS

- ½ cup (54 g) panko breadcrumbs
- 1 egg
- 8 ounces (227 g) shrimp, peeled, deveined, and tails removed
- 2 hoagie rolls
- 2 tablespoons (28 g) mayo
- Sliced tomatoes
- Shredded lettuce
- Oil spray

DIRECTIONS

1. In a large bowl, stir together the mayo, chili sauce, and Sriracha. Cover and set aside in the refrigerator.

2. In a shallow bowl, add the panko. In another shallow bowl, beat the egg.

3. Preheat the air fryer to 400° F (200° C). Pat the shrimp dry, then dip each shrimp into the egg, then into the panko to coat. Place the shrimp in the air fryer, spray with oil, and cook for 8-12 minutes, flipping halfway through.

4. Add the shrimp into the sauce mixture, carefully stirring until fully coated.

5. Assemble the sandwiches with mayo, tomato, lettuce, and shrimp. Serve immediately.

POBLANO & PEPPER JACK PORK BURGER

The classic burger gets reimagined! Roasted poblano peppers and onions are served on a juicy pork burger and topped with a melty pepper jack cheese sauce. This delicious burger offers a mild heat that anyone will enjoy, whether you like spice or not!

COOK TIME: 26 MIN | EFFORT: EASY

INGREDIENTS

- 1   poblano pepper, sliced
- 1   small onion, sliced
- 8   ounces (227 g) ground pork
- ½   teaspoon garlic powder
- ½   teaspoon onion powder
- ½   teaspoon salt
- ¼   teaspoon pepper
- 2   brioche buns
-     Oil spray

SAUCE

- 3   tablespoons (42 g) mayo
- ½   cup (59 g) shredded pepper Jack cheese
- ¼   teaspoon salt
- ¼   teaspoon pepper
- ¼   teaspoon onion powder
- ¼   teaspoon garlic powder

DIRECTIONS

1. Preheat the air fryer to 400° F (200° C). Add the pepper and onions to the air fryer, spray with oil, and cook for 12-16 minutes, shaking halfway through.

2. In a small bowl, combine the ground pork, garlic powder, onion powder, salt, and pepper. Divide the mixture into two patties. Spray the air fryer with oil and add the patties. Cook for 6-10 minutes, flipping halfway through.

3. Meanwhile, in a small bowl, combine the mayo, cheese, salt, pepper, onion powder, and garlic powder. Divide the mixture on top of the two pork patties and cook for 2-4 minutes or until melted.

4. Place each patty onto a bun and top with the pepper and onion mixture. Serve immediately.

MEATLESS
MAINS

Incorporating more vegetables into your diet is never a bad idea; making them delicious and easy? Even better! With meals like eggplant Parmesan, pot pie, stromboli, quiche, and soups (yes, I said soups!), you won't be missing the meat. These meatless mains showcase vegetables in the best ways possible!

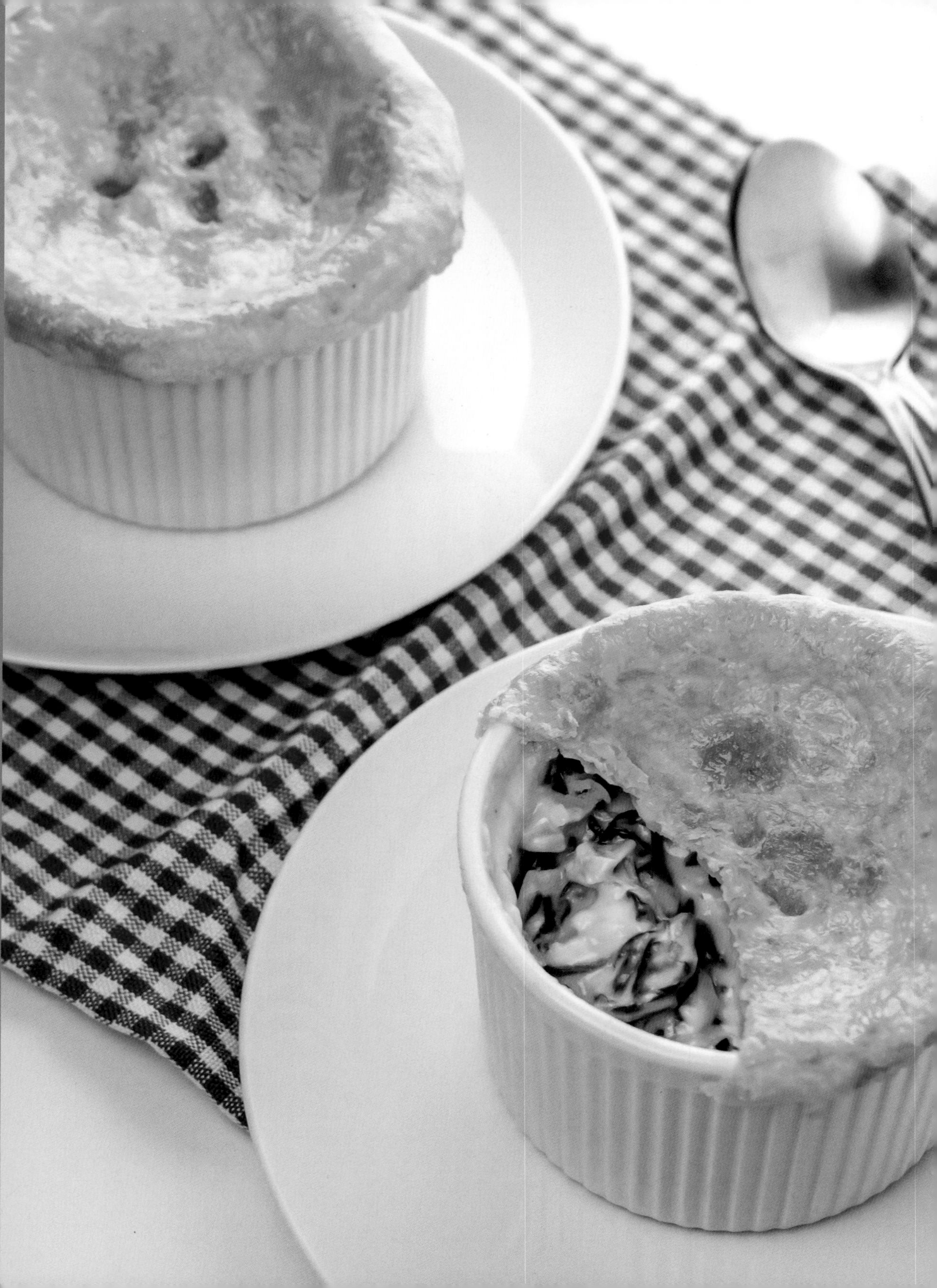

SPINACH AND ARTICHOKE POT PIES

Step aside chicken pot pie, there's a new dinner in town! I gave one of my favorite appetizers a fun, main-entree makeover by taking everything I love about spinach and artichoke dip and turning it into fun individual-sized pot pies. The crisp top mixed with the creamy interior is a match made in heaven!

COOK TIME: 12 MIN | EFFORT: MODERATE

INGREDIENTS

- 2 tablespoons (28 g) butter
- 2 tablespoons (16 g) flour
- 1 cup (227 ml) milk
- 6 ounces (170 g) fresh spinach
- 2 garlic cloves, minced
- 2 tablespoons (12 g) grated Parmesan cheese
- ½ teaspoon onion powder
- ½ teaspoon salt
- ¼ teaspoon pepper
- 6 ounces (170 g) marinated artichokes, chopped

PASTRY

- ½ cup (64 g) flour
- 3 tablespoons (42 g) butter
- 2 tablespoons (30 ml) water, ice-cold
- ¼ teaspoon salt, optional
- 1 egg mixed with 1 tablespoon (15 ml) water, optional

DIRECTIONS

1. In a small saucepan over medium heat, melt the butter. Whisk in the flour, stirring continuously for 2 minutes. Gradually, add in the milk, stirring after each addition. Add in the spinach, stirring until wilted and incorporated, then stir in the garlic, Parmesan, onion powder, salt, pepper, and artichokes; set aside.

2. Preheat the air fryer to 390° F (190° C).

3. In a small bowl, using your fingers, combine the flour and butter until the mixture resembles coarse crumbs. Gradually, add the water, while stirring with a fork, until a dough forms. Divide the dough into two even-sized balls. On a lightly floured surface, roll each dough ball into a 9-inch circle.

4. Evenly pour the mixture into two greased 10-ounce ramekins. Top each ramekin with pastry dough, cut three slits into the tops, and, optionally, brush with the egg mixture. Carefully, place the pot pies in the air fryer and cook for 10 minutes. Serve immediately.

ROASTED VEGETABLE & CHEDDAR QUICHE

While perhaps thought more of as a brunch item than the main entree for dinner, quiche has all the makings of a delicious and satisfying meal. Loaded with protein (thanks to the eggs) and tons of roasted vegetables, this quiche may become a fixture in your dinner routine.

COOK TIME: 1 HR 5 MIN | EFFORT: MODERATE

INGREDIENTS

1	small green pepper, diced
½	small onion, diced
6	asparagus spears, cut into fourths
3	ounces (85 g) tomatoes, halved
1	prepared pie crust
4	eggs
¼	cup (60 ml) milk
¼	cup (28 g) shredded cheddar cheese
½	teaspoon salt
¼	teaspoon pepper
	Oil spray

DIRECTIONS

1. Preheat the air fryer to 400° F (200° C).

2. Add the peppers, onions, asparagus, and tomatoes to the air fryer, spray with oil, and cook for 14-18 minutes, stirring halfway through. Set aside to cool.

3. Meanwhile, in a 6-inch springform pan, carefully press the pie dough to the bottom and up the sides of the pan. Firmly pressing areas of overlap. Line the pie dough with parchment paper and fill it with pie weights or dried beans to keep the edges from falling down. Place the pan in the air fryer and cook for 8-12 minutes, or until the crust holds its shape without the weights.

4. Reduce the air fryer temperature to 340° F (170° C).

5. In a medium bowl, whisk together the eggs and milk. Stir in the cheese, roasted vegetables, salt, and pepper. Carefully, pour the mixture into the pie shell and cover with foil. Place in the air fryer and bake for 28-32 minutes, remove the foil and bake another 8-12 minutes, until the quiche is set in the center. Carefully remove from the pan and allow to cool 10-15 minutes before slicing and serving.

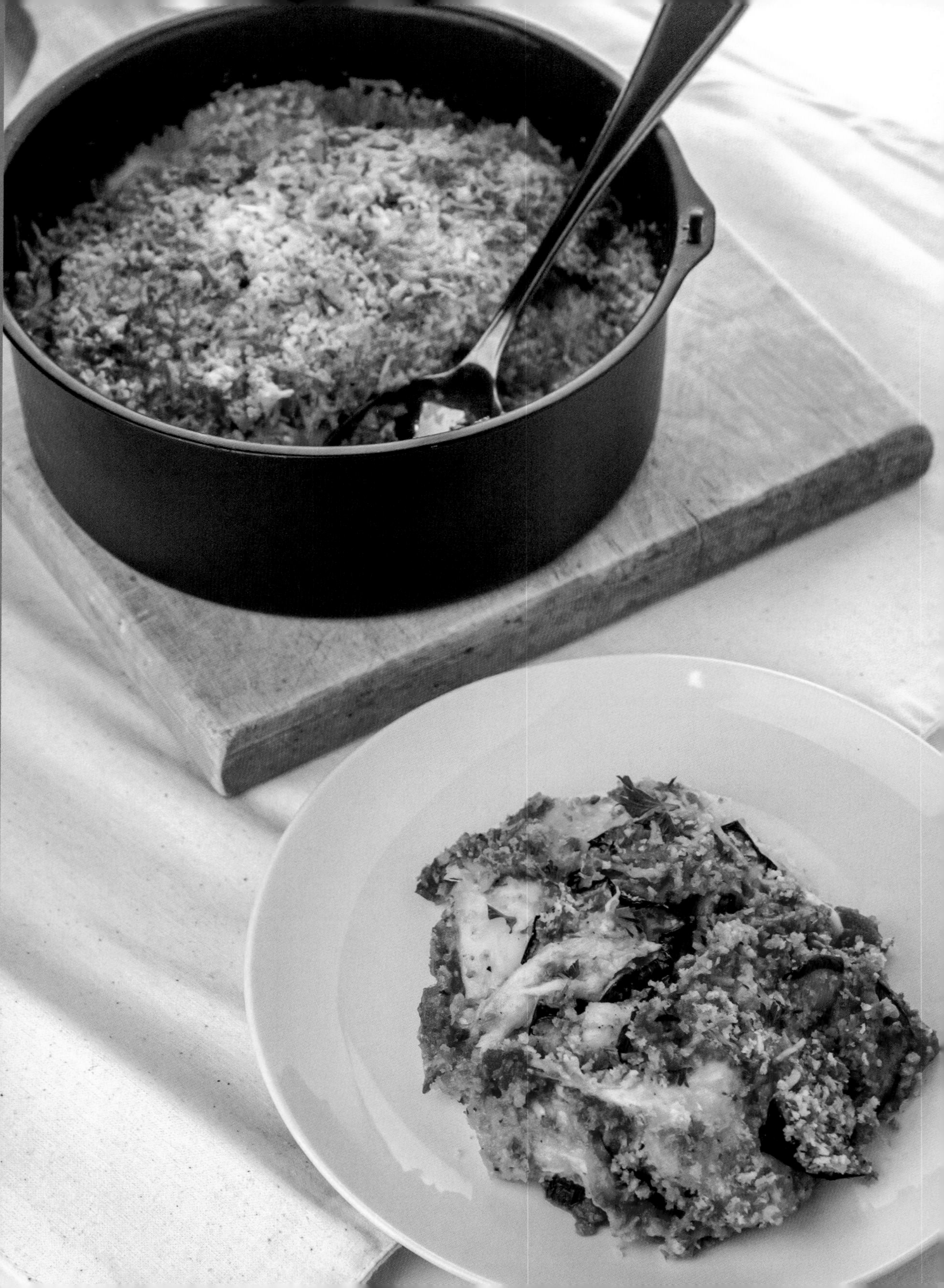

DEEP-DISH BAKED EGGPLANT PARMESAN

All the ingredients of eggplant Parmesan, but layered like lasagna! It's not only beautiful, but also a much easier (and healthier) way to make it. No frying and no breading, just layers of melty cheese, crispy bread crumbs, roasted eggplant, and of course, marinara! Just because it's simple, doesn't mean it lacks in flavor in the slightest!

COOK TIME: 28 MIN | EFFORT: EASY

INGREDIENTS

- 1 large eggplant, sliced ¼-inch (0.5 cm) thick
- 1 teaspoon salt
- ½ teaspoon pepper
- ¾ cup (81 g) panko breadcrumbs
- ½ teaspoon Italian seasoning
- ¼ teaspoon onion powder
- ¼ teaspoon garlic powder
- 1 teaspoon canola oil
- 1½ cups (338 g) marinara sauce
- 8 ounces (227 g) fresh mozzarella, thinly sliced
- ¼ cup (24 g) grated Parmesan cheese
- Oil spray

DIRECTIONS

1. Preheat the air fryer to 400° F (200° C). Spray the air fryer with oil and arrange the eggplant slices. Spray the eggplant, season with salt and pepper, and cook for 14-18 minutes. Carefully flipping halfway through.

2. In a medium bowl, combine the panko, Italian seasoning, onion powder, garlic powder, and oil.

3. Spray a 6-inch baking dish with oil and pour half of the marinara on the bottom. Layer on half of the eggplant, cheese, and prepared breadcrumbs. Repeat layering with remaining ingredients. Cover with foil, cook for 8-12 minutes, removing foil halfway through. Serve on its own or with garlic bread or a salad.

TOMATO AND SPINACH STUFFED STROMBOLI

Stromboli is similar to calzones but rolled instead of folded over. Filled with nutritious vegetables and melty cheese, this is as beautiful as it is satisfying! The best part is it's all made from scratch, even the dough! And don't be intimidated by making a yeast dough, this one is as easy as they come!

COOK TIME: 30 MIN | EFFORT: MODERATE

DOUGH

¾	cup (180 ml) warm water
1	tablespoon (12 g) sugar
1	packet (2¼ teaspoons [6 g]) active dry yeast
2	tablespoons (30 ml) canola oil
1	teaspoon salt
2	cups (240 g) flour

INGREDIENTS

1	tablespoon (15 ml) canola oil
1	small onion, thinly sliced
1	small green pepper, thinly sliced
1	garlic clove, minced
1	tablespoon (2 g) Italian seasoning
1	teaspoon salt
½	teaspoon pepper
¼	teaspoon red pepper flakes
6	ounces (170 g) fresh baby spinach
1	(14.5-ounce [411 g]) can diced tomatoes
1	cup (113 g) shredded mozzarella cheese
1	egg mixed with 1 tablespoon (15 ml) water, optional
2	teaspoons (6 g) sesame seeds, optional
	Marinara sauce, optional for dipping

DIRECTIONS

1. In a medium bowl, combine the water, sugar, and yeast. Allow the mixture to sit for 5 minutes, once foamy, add the oil, salt, and flour. Stir the mixture until a dough forms. Transfer the dough to a clean, greased bowl. Cover with plastic wrap and allow to rise for 1 hour or until doubled in size.

2. Meanwhile, in a large skillet over medium-high heat, warm the oil. Add the onion and cook until softened, about 5 minutes. Add the green pepper and cook until softened, about 3-5 minutes. Add the garlic, Italian seasoning, salt, pepper, and red pepper flakes, cooking for 1 minute. Add the spinach, stirring until wilted, then add the tomatoes. Cook for 3-5 minutes, until slightly reduced, then remove from heat.

3. Preheat the air fryer to 350° F (170° C).

4. Transfer the dough to a floured surface and knead a few times. Roll the dough into a roughly 15x15-inch square, about ¼-inch thick. Cut the dough down the middle to make two rectangles. Sprinkle each half with cheese and spread the spinach mixture on top. Starting from the long side, roll the dough up, tucking the ends under and pinching to seal the seams. Optionally, brush the dough with the egg mixture and top with sesame seeds. Using a sharp knife, score four vents into the tops of each stromboli.

5. Carefully, line the air fryer with parchment paper and add the stromboli, cooking one at a time, and cook for 13-17 minutes, until crispy and a light golden color. Repeat with the second stromboli. Slice and serve with marinara.

ARUGULA & CHEDDAR EGG SOUFFLÉS

They sound fancy, they look fancy, and they taste fancy but these cheddar and arugula soufflés don't take tons of effort to make. One bite and you'll be hooked! But don't stop there, try it again with different cheeses and greens to make it your own.

COOK TIME: 18 MIN | EFFORT: EASY

INGREDIENTS

- 2 tablespoons (28 g) butter
- 2 tablespoons (16 g) flour
- ½ cup (113 ml) milk
- 1 teaspoon Dijon mustard
- ½ teaspoon salt
- ¼ teaspoon pepper
- 2 eggs, separated
- ½ cup (66 g) cheddar cheese
- 1 handful arugula
- ¼ teaspoon cream of tartar

DIRECTIONS

1. In a small saucepan over medium-low heat, melt the butter. Add the flour, whisking for 2 minutes. Gradually, pour in the milk, whisking continuously until thickened. Add the mustard, salt, and pepper. Quickly whisk in the egg yolks and cheese until melted. Remove from heat and stir in the arugula; set aside.

2. Preheat the air fryer to 330° F (160° C).

3. In a large clean bowl, using a hand mixer with clean beaters, beat together the egg whites and cream of tartar until stiff peaks form.

4. Fold ⅓ of the whites into the cooled cheese mixture. Carefully fold the cheese mixture into the remaining whites. Evenly pour the mixture into two greased 10-ounce ramekins. Place them in the air fryer and cook for 12-16 minutes, until lightly browned and puffed up. Serve immediately.

FALAFEL SLIDERS WITH CREAMY DILL SAUCE

Falafels make for an already delicious appetizer or entree but I had the thought one day, "Why not make them into sliders?" And that's how we landed here! Served with fresh vegetables and a creamy herb sauce, I have no doubt you'll be making these again!

COOK TIME: 16 MIN | EFFORT: EASY

SAUCE

- 2 tablespoons (28 g) mayo
- 2 tablespoons (30 g) plain yogurt
- 1 teaspoon lemon juice
- ¼ teaspoon salt
- ⅛ teaspoon pepper
- ¼ teaspoon dried dill weed
- 1 garlic clove, minced

INGREDIENTS

- 1 (15-ounce) can chickpeas, drained
- ½ small red onion, roughly chopped (about ½ cup), slice remaining for serving
- 3 garlic cloves, roughly chopped
- 3 tablespoons (24 g) flour
- 2 tablespoons (5 g) chopped parsley
- 1 teaspoon ground cumin
- 1 teaspoon ground coriander
- ⅛ teaspoon ground cardamom
- 1 teaspoon salt
- ¼ teaspoon pepper
- 6 slider buns
- 1 small tomato, sliced for serving
- 1 small cucumber, sliced for serving
  Oil spray

DIRECTIONS

1. In a small bowl, stir together the mayo, yogurt, lemon juice, salt, pepper, dill, and garlic. Cover and refrigerate.

2. Preheat the air fryer to 350° F (170° C).

3. In a food processor fitted with an 'S' blade, add the chickpeas, onions, garlic, flour, parsley, cumin, coriander, cardamom, salt, and pepper. Pulse until a coarse meal forms, being careful not to let the mixture become a paste. Using your hands, carefully form the mixture into six even disks.

4. Spray the air fryer with oil, add the falafel, spray with oil, and cook for 12-16 minutes, flipping halfway through and spraying with oil. Serve on slider buns topped with sauce, onion, tomato, and cucumber.

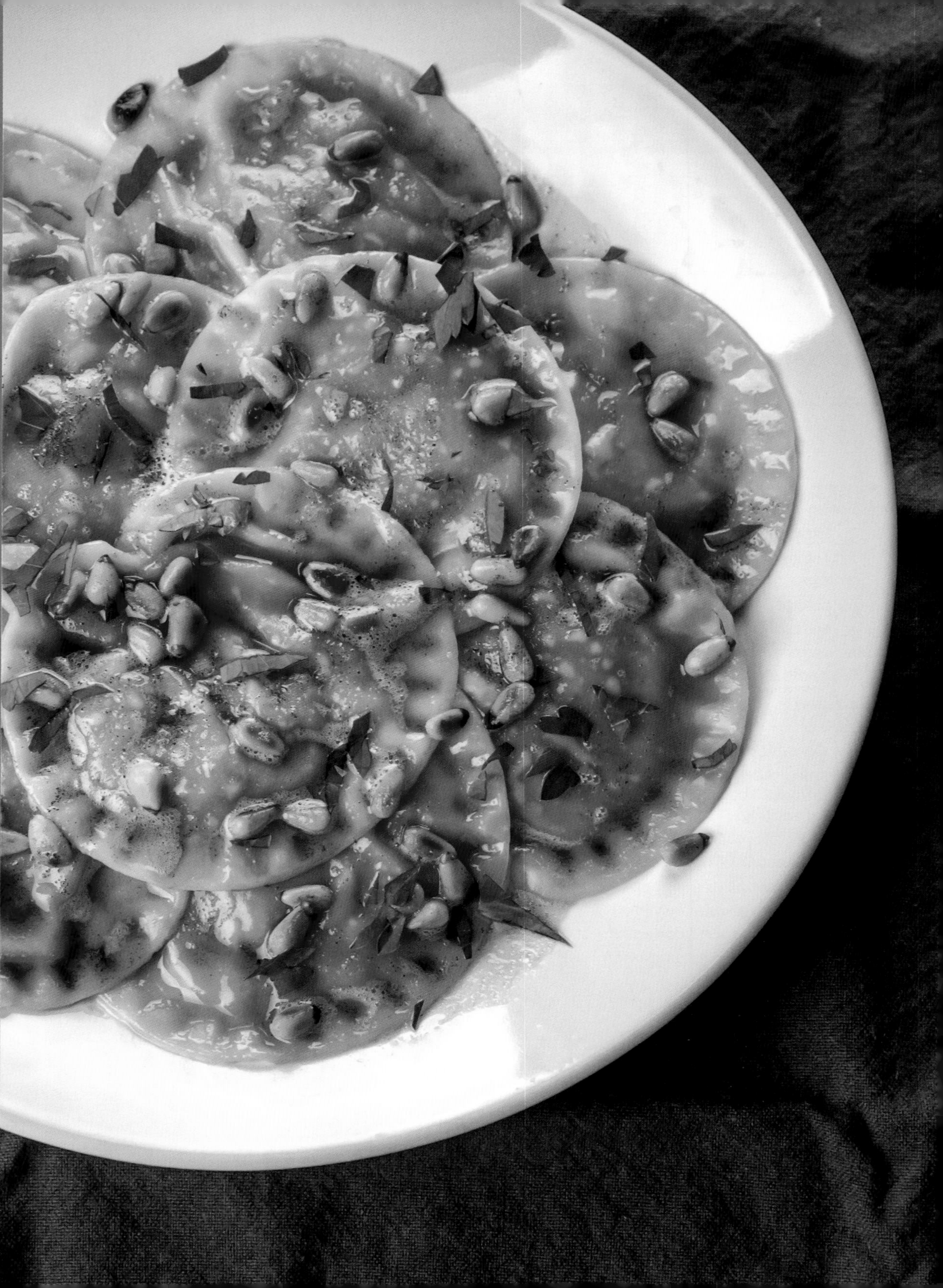

SWEET POTATO RAVIOLI

While the air fryer can be used to cook your entire dinner, it's often overlooked when it comes to getting dinner on the table quicker. For this recipe, the air fryer roasts some delicious sweet potato which then gets transformed into a delicious ravioli served with browned butter. It's both rich and delicious!

COOK TIME: 1 HR 10 MIN | EFFORT: MODERATE

INGREDIENTS

- 2 medium sweet potatoes
- 2 tablespoons (12 g) grated Parmesan cheese, plus more for serving
- ½ teaspoon dried parsley
  Pinch grated nutmeg
- ¼ teaspoon salt
- ⅛ teaspoon pepper
- ½ teaspoon onion powder
- ¼ teaspoon garlic powder
- 1 tablespoon (8 g) flour
- 1 package wonton wrappers
- 1 stick (113 g) butter
- 2 tablespoons (17 g) pine nuts, toasted

DIRECTIONS

1. Preheat the air fryer to 390° F (190° C). Using a knife, pierce the sweet potatoes several times. Add the potatoes to the air fryer and cook for 40-50 minutes, flipping halfway through. Carefully remove the skins from the sweet potatoes.

2. In a large bowl, combine the potatoes, Parmesan, parsley, nutmeg, salt, pepper, onion powder, garlic powder, and flour until smooth.

3. Bring a large pot of water to a boil.

4. Meanwhile, place two wonton wrappers on a work surface. Using a tablespoon, scoop a level spoonful of the potato mixture into the middle of one wrapper. Brush water along the edges of the wrapper. Place the second wrapper on top and lightly press the edges to seal. Leave the ravioli as is, or cut into circles with a cup or pasta cutter. Repeat with remaining wonton wrappers until all filling is used.

5. Reduce water to a simmer, and gently place 12-15 ravioli in the water, gently stirring. Cook for 2-4 minutes, until they begin to float. Carefully remove the ravioli with a slotted spoon and transfer to a greased tray.

6. In a large pan over medium heat, melt the butter, stirring continuously. The butter will begin to foam, cook for about 5-8 minutes, until it turns golden brown (be very careful that it doesn't burn). You'll notice a nutty and strong butter smell. Remove from heat, add the ravioli, and spoon the butter over the ravioli. Serve topped with pine nuts.

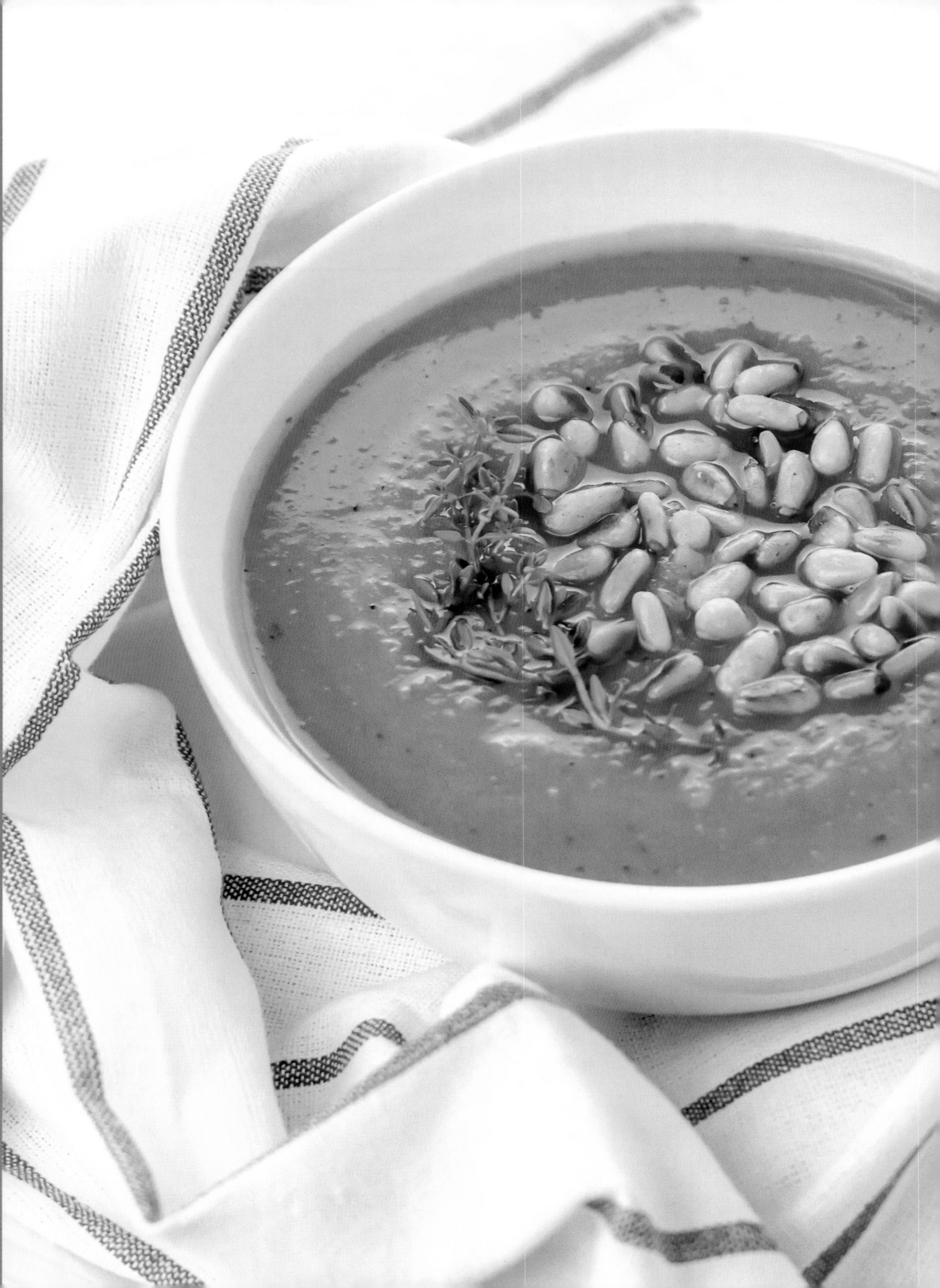

ROASTED BUTTERNUT SQUASH SOUP

Thick-skinned and often difficult to peel, butternut squash is indeed worth the effort. But what if I told you, that effort is completely unnecessary? It's true! Just put the squash in the air fryer and roast it whole. When it's done the skin peels away with ease and is quickly transformed into this fantastic fall soup!

COOK TIME: 35 MIN | EFFORT: EASY

INGREDIENTS

- 1 (1-pound [452 g]) butternut squash
- 1 small onion, diced
- 1 (15-ounce [444 ml]) can vegetable broth
- ½ teaspoon dried thyme
- ½ teaspoon salt
- ¼ teaspoon pepper
- 2 ounces (57 g) pine nuts, toasted
  Oil spray

DIRECTIONS

1. Preheat the air fryer to 360° F (180° C). Using a knife, pierce the squash several times. Add the squash to the air fryer and cook for 20 minutes. Add the onion to the air fryer, spray with oil, and cook for an additional 10 minutes.

2. Carefully peel the skin off the squash, slice in half, remove its ends, scoop out its seeds, and chop. In a blender, add the squash, onion, broth, thyme, salt, and pepper. Blending until smooth.

3. In a medium saucepan over medium heat, pour in the soup, bring to a simmer, and cook for 3-5 minutes, until heated through. Serve topped with toasted pine nuts.

ROASTED RED PEPPER SOUP WITH CROUTONS

Roasting vegetables brings out their natural sweetness and I love the flavor that a little charing adds. The air fryer does a great job at roasting vegetables and is your express ticket to this robust-flavored soup that come together with ease!

COOK TIME: 40 MIN | EFFORT: EASY

INGREDIENTS

- 4 red peppers, seeds removed and quartered
- 1 large onion, diced
- ½ teaspoon salt
- ¼ teaspoon pepper
- 2 tablespoons (28 g) butter
- 3 garlic cloves, minced
- ¼ teaspoon dried basil
- ¼ teaspoon dried oregano
- 2½ cups (591 ml) vegetable broth
- 1 teaspoon low-sodium soy sauce
- 1 teaspoon onion powder
- ½ teaspoons garlic powder
- 2 dashes Worcestershire sauce
- ½ cup (118 ml) half & half

CROUTONS

- 1 French baguette, cubed
- 1 teaspoon canola oil
- ½ teaspoon garlic powder
- 1 teaspoon Italian seasoning
- Oil spray

DIRECTIONS

1. Preheat the air fryer to 400° F (200° C). Add the peppers and onions to the air fryer, spray with oil, and season with salt and pepper. Cook for 13-17 minutes, stirring halfway through. Set aside to cool.

2. In a large pot over medium heat, melt the butter. Add the peppers, onions, garlic, basil, oregano, broth, soy sauce, onion powder, garlic powder, and Worcestershire sauce, stirring to combine. Bring to a boil then reduce to a simmer, cover, and cook for 20 minutes, stirring occasionally.

3. Meanwhile, in a medium bowl, combine the bread cubes, oil, garlic powder, and Italian seasoning, tossing to coat. Place the bread cubes into the air fryer and cook for 5-7 minutes, until toasted.

4. Meanwhile, using an immersion blender, blend the soup until smooth. Stir in the half & half, cooking for 5 minutes to heat through. Serve topped with croutons.

NOTE: If you do not have an immersion blender, you can use a stand blender or food processor to puree the soup, then return to the pot and reheat before adding the half & half.

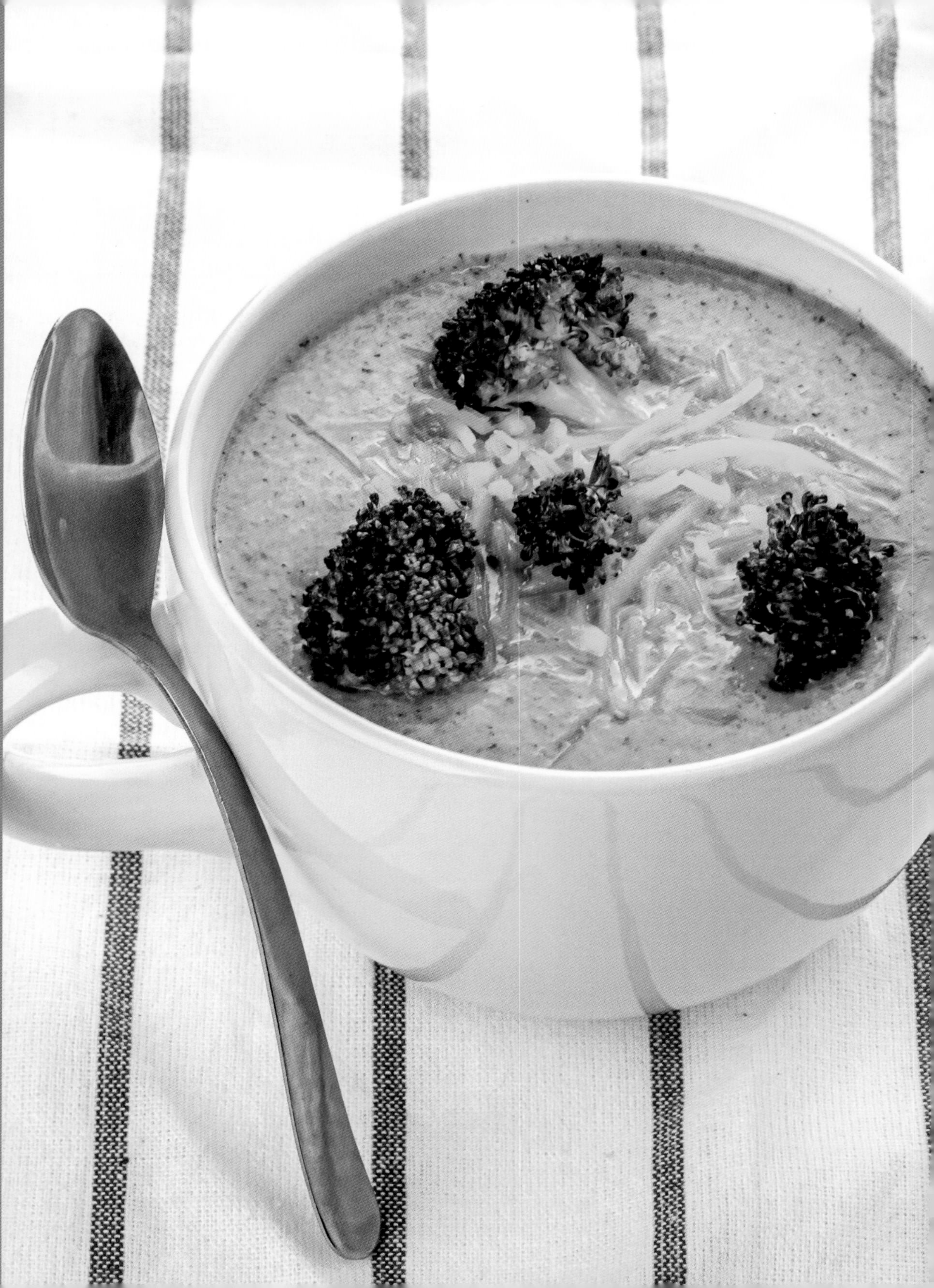

ROASTED BROCCOLI AND CHEESE SOUP

You've probably had broccoli cheddar soup at one point or another but have you ever had it with roasted broccoli? Probably not and I think that's a darn shame. The roasted broccoli adds a robust and slightly smoky flavor to this creamy soup that I think is irresistible!

COOK TIME: 35 MIN | EFFORT: EASY

INGREDIENTS

- 1 pound (452 g) broccoli, cut into small florets
- 1 medium onion, diced
- ½ teaspoon garlic powder
- ¼ teaspoon onion powder
- ½ teaspoon salt
- ½ teaspoon pepper
- 1 tablespoon (15 ml) canola oil
- 2 garlic cloves, minced
- 3 cups (709 ml) vegetable broth
- 1 cup (237 ml) half & half
- 8 ounces (227 g) sharp cheddar cheese
- 2 tablespoons (12 g) grated Parmesan cheese
- Oil spray

DIRECTIONS

1. Preheat the air fryer to 370° F (180° C). Add the broccoli and onions to the air fryer, spray with oil, and season with garlic powder, onion powder, salt, and pepper. Cook for 8-12 minutes, stirring halfway through, until browned. Reserve ½ cup of broccoli when finished.

2. In a large saucepan over medium-high heat, warm the oil. Add the garlic and cook for 1 minute, until fragrant. Add the broth and bring to a simmer. Add the cooked broccoli and onions to the broth; simmer for 15 minutes.

3. Using an immersion blender, blend until smooth. Stir in the half & half, cheddar, and Parmesan. Cook for 5 minutes more, stirring continuously until the cheese is fully melted. Serve each bowl with the reserved broccoli on top.

NOTE: If you do not have an immersion blender, you can use a stand blender or food processor to puree the soup, then return to the pot and reheat before adding the half & half and cheese.

SPICE UP
YOUR LIFE

Turn up the flavors and explore these south-of-the-border dishes right in your kitchen! With familiar entrees like fajitas, tacos, and enchiladas to more adventurous meals like chile rellenos and beef empanadas. You'll feel like you're eating at your favorite Mexican restaurant without ever leaving the house!

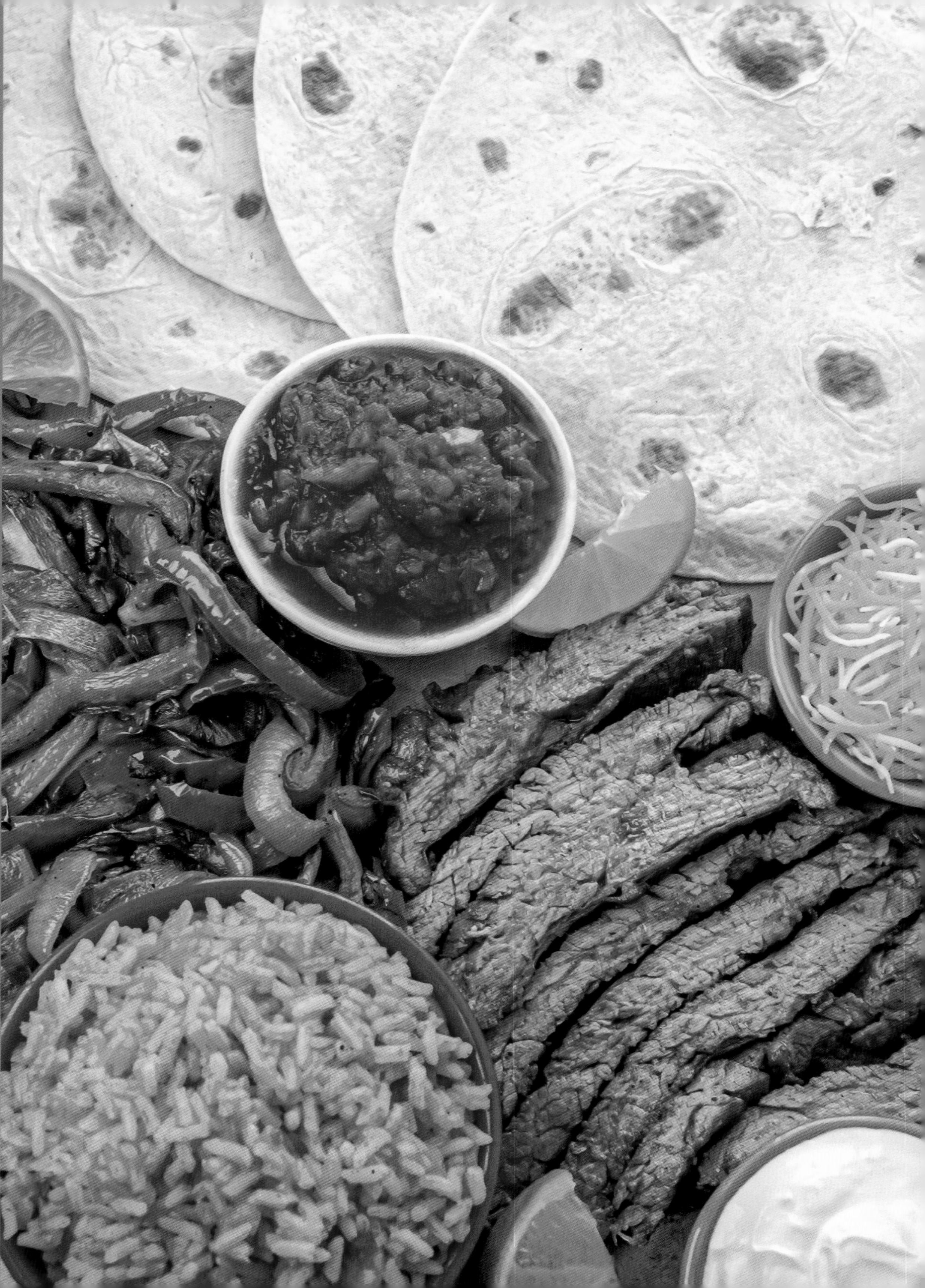

MARINATED SKIRT STEAK FAJITAS

While perhaps not authentically Mexican, I couldn't fathom the idea of not having these steak fajitas in this book. They come together with such ease, they only need a quick soak in a flavorful marinade and you're on the fast track to a delicious steak fajita dinner for two!

COOK TIME: 20 MIN | EFFORT: EASY

INGREDIENTS

- 2 tablespoons (30 ml) pineapple juice
- 1 tablespoon (15 ml) lime juice
- 2 teaspoon (10 ml) canola oil
- 2 teaspoon (10 ml) low-sodium soy sauce
- 1 garlic clove, minced
- 1 (8-ounce [227 g]) skirt steak
- 1 teaspoon chili powder
- ½ teaspoon ground cumin
- ½ teaspoon paprika
- ¼ teaspoon salt, if desired
- ¼ teaspoon pepper
- 1 small pepper, sliced
- 1 small onion, sliced
  Oil spray
- 6 (6-inch) tortillas
  Shredded cheese, of choice
  Sour cream
  Salsa

DIRECTIONS

1. In a large bowl, stir together the pineapple juice, lime juice, oil, soy sauce, and garlic, add the steak and marinate for 1 hour. Remove from the marinade, pat dry, and season with chili powder, cumin, paprika, salt, and pepper.

2. Preheat the air fryer to 400° F (200° C). Add the peppers and onions to the air fryer, spray with oil, and cook for 8-12 minutes. Stir the mixture, add the steak, and cook for 4-8 minutes more, stirring again halfway through. Let the steak rest for 10 minutes before slicing.

3. Serve the sliced steak with tortillas, roasted vegetables, cheese, sour cream, and salsa.

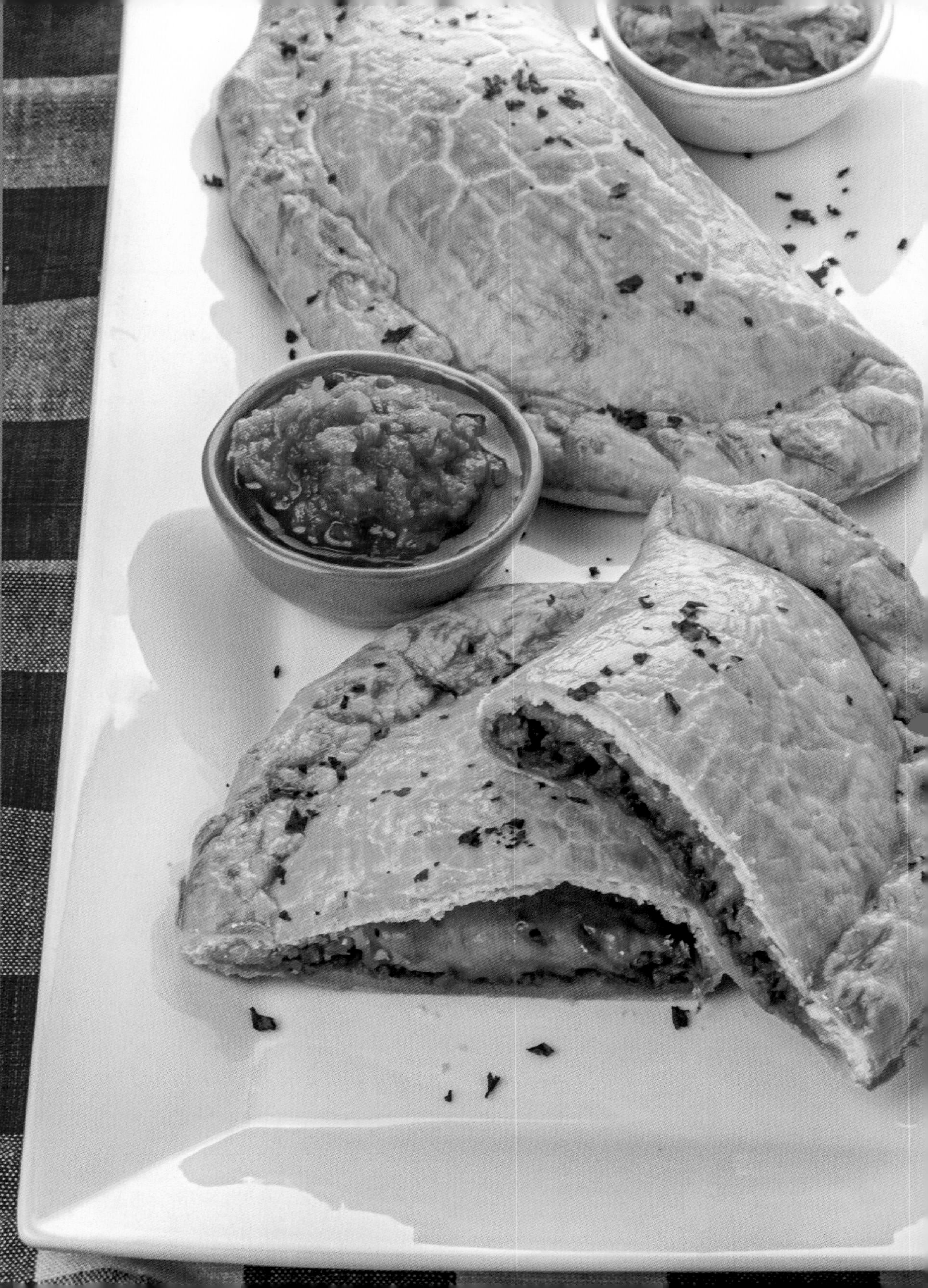

SEASONED BEEF AND CHEESE EMPANADAS

With ingredients you probably already have on hand, you can transform ground beef into a show-stopping handheld dinner. These beef empanadas are literally packed with flavor and, honestly, make for a fun way to serve dinner!

COOK TIME: 30 MIN | EFFORT: EASY

DOUGH

- 1½ cups (180 g) flour
- ½ cup (113 g) butter, cubed
- ⅓ cup (75 ml) water, ice-cold

FILLING

- 1 tablespoon (15 ml) canola oil
- 1 small onion, chopped
- 1 clove garlic, minced
- 8 ounces (227 g) ground beef
- 1 tablespoon (11 g) tomato paste
- ½ teaspoon dried oregano
- ½ teaspoon ground cumin
- ½ teaspoon chili powder
- ½ teaspoon paprika
- ½ teaspoon salt
- ¼ teaspoon pepper
- 2 tablespoons (30 ml) salsa
- 1 cup (118 g) shredded Monterey Jack
- 1 egg, beaten with 1 tablespoon (15 ml) water
- Oil spray

TOPPINGS

- Cilantro, chopped, for garnish
- Salsa, for serving
- Guacamole, for serving

DIRECTIONS

1. In a small bowl, using your fingers, combine the flour and butter until the mixture resembles coarse crumbs. Gradually add the water, while stirring with a fork, until a dough forms. Divide the dough into two even-sized balls, cover, and refrigerate.

2. In a large pan over medium-high heat, warm the oil. Add the onion and garlic, cooking for 5-7 minutes until the onions are translucent. Add the beef and cook for 5 minutes, until no longer pink. Add the tomato paste, oregano, cumin, chili powder, paprika, salt, pepper, and salsa, cooking for another 5 minutes. Remove from the heat and let it cool to room temperature.

3. Preheat the air fryer to 400° F (200° C). On a lightly floured surface, roll each dough ball into a 9-inch circle. Spoon the meat mixture into the center of each circle and top each half with cheese. Fold the dough over the mixture, crimp the edges, and brush each empanada with the egg mixture. Carefully line the air fryer with parchment paper and add an empanada, cooking one at a time, for 8-12 minutes or until crispy and a light golden color.

4. Serve topped with cilantro and salsa, and guacamole on the side for dipping.

MEXICAN SHREDDED CHICKEN TAQUITOS

Tonight's dinner is as easy as 1-2-3. Shredded chicken is rolled into crispy tortillas and melty cheese making for a fun-textured, flavor-rich dinner. The air fryer does double duty with this recipe, you'll cook the chicken and crisp the taquitos in it!

COOK TIME: 16 MIN | EFFORT: EASY

INGREDIENTS

1	garlic clove, minced
1	teaspoon chili powder
½	teaspoon paprika
½	teaspoon dried oregano
½	teaspoon ground cumin
¼	teaspoon pepper
¼	teaspoon salt
1	teaspoon canola oil
8	ounces (227 g) boneless skinless chicken thighs
½	cup (41 g) shredded Mexican cheese blend
4	(6-inch) tortillas
	Oil spray

TOPPINGS

Guacamole

Sour cream

Salsa

Pickled onions, recipe on our website!

DIRECTIONS

1. Preheat the air fryer to 380º F (190º C).

2. In a resealable bag, combine the garlic, chili powder, paprika, oregano, cumin, pepper, and salt. Add the chicken and shake to coat. Spray the air fryer with oil, add the chicken, spray with oil, and cook for 12-16 minutes, flipping halfway through. Let the chicken rest for 10 minutes before shredding.

3. Fill each tortilla evenly with the shredded chicken, 2 tablespoons of cheese, and roll closed. Spray the air fryer with oil, add the taquitos, seam side down, spray with oil, and cook for 6-10 minutes, flipping halfway through. Serve with toppings of choice.

TRY YOUR OWN PICKLED ONIONS
https://bestrecipes.co/recipes/pickled-onions

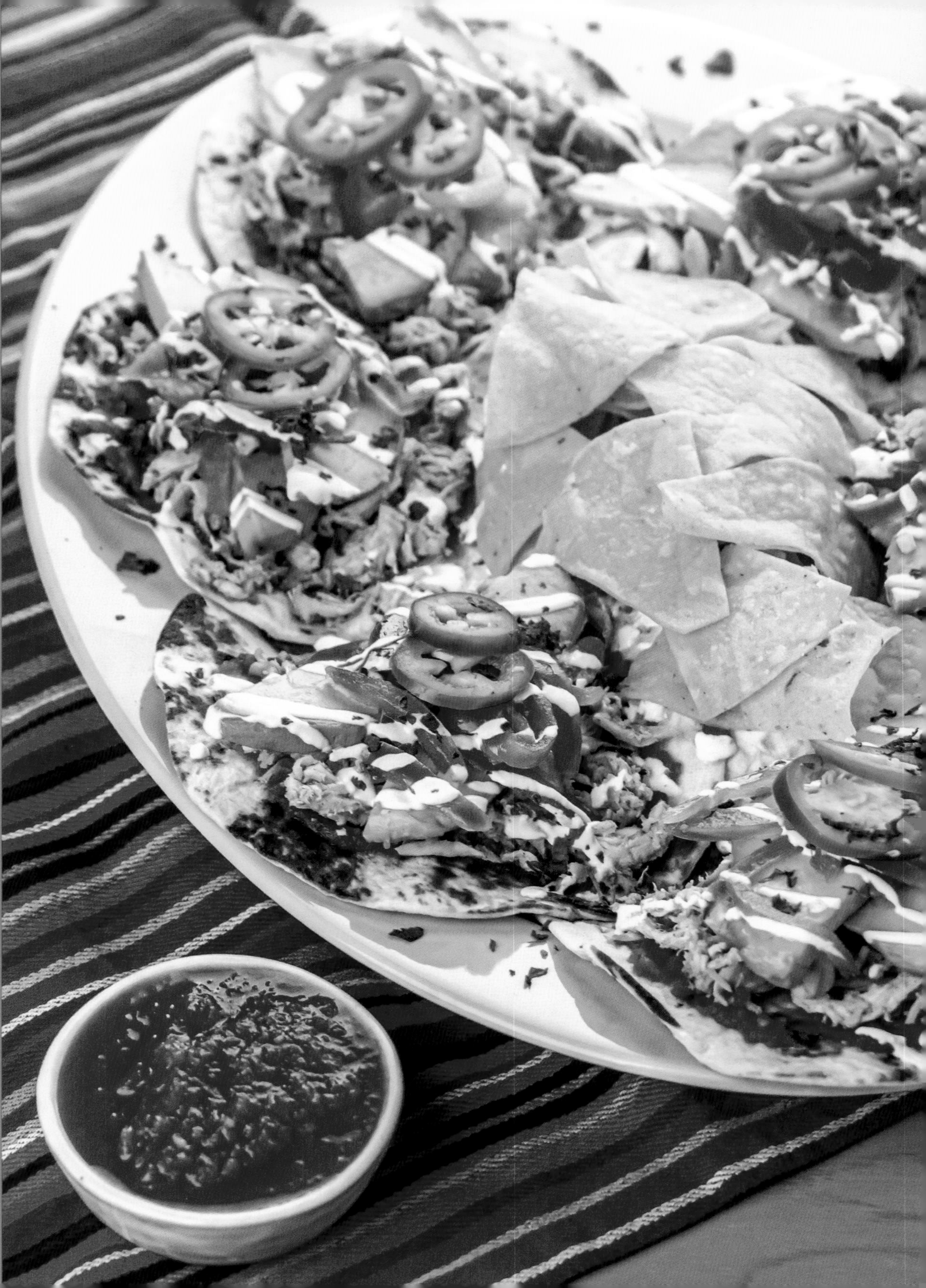

STREET STYLE CHICKEN TACOS

Roasted chicken thighs are shredded and used for the filling in these classic chicken tacos. Serve them up with your favorite toppings and enjoy your taco Tuesday, or Wednesday, or any day!

COOK TIME: 16 MIN | EFFORT: EASY

INGREDIENTS

1	clove garlic, minced
1	teaspoon chili powder
½	teaspoon paprika
½	teaspoon dried oregano
½	teaspoon ground cumin
¼	teaspoon pepper
¼	teaspoon salt
1	teaspoon canola oil
8	ounces (227 g) boneless skinless chicken thighs
	Oil spray
6	(6-inch) tortillas

TOPPINGS

Salsa
Avocado
Jalapeño
Pickled Onions, check out our website for the recipe!
Sour cream
Cilantro

DIRECTIONS

1. Preheat the air fryer to 380° F (190° C).

2. In a resealable bag, combine the garlic, chili powder, paprika, oregano, cumin, pepper, and salt. Add the chicken and shake to coat. Spray the air fryer with oil, add the chicken, spray with oil, and cook for 12-16 minutes, flipping halfway through. Let the chicken rest for 10 minutes before shredding.

3. Serve the chicken on a tortilla, topped with salsa, avocado, jalapeño, pickled onions, sour cream, and cilantro.

TRY YOUR OWN PICKLED ONIONS
https://bestrecipes.co/recipes/pickled-onions

TEX MEX STUFFED PEPPERS

A comfort food classic gets a tex-mex makeover! All of the familiar ingredients of stuffed peppers are here but with a little twist. Seasoned with taco seasoning and filled to the brim with rice, beef, black beans, and shredded cheese, you're in for a world of flavor perfect for any night!

COOK TIME: 14 MIN | EFFORT: EASY

INGREDIENTS

- 4   medium green peppers, cored
- 1   tablespoon (15 ml) canola oil
- 8   ounces (227 g) ground beef
- 1   tablespoon (11 g) tomato paste
- ½   teaspoon dried oregano
- ½   teaspoon ground cumin
- ½   teaspoon chili powder
- ½   teaspoon paprika
- ½   teaspoon salt
- ¼   teaspoon pepper
- 1   (15-ounce [444 g]) can corn, drained
- 1   (15-ounce [444 g]) can black beans, drained
- 1   (15-ounce [444 g]) can diced tomatoes with green chilies
- 1   cup (195 g) cooked rice
-   Oil spray
- ½   cup (41 g) shredded Mexican blend cheese

DIRECTIONS

1. Place the peppers in the air fryer, spray with oil, and cook at 380º F (190º C) for 10 minutes.

2. Meanwhile, in a large pan over medium heat, warm the oil. Add the ground beef and cook for 5-7 minutes, until no longer pink. Add the tomato paste, oregano, cumin, chili powder, paprika, salt, and pepper, stirring together and cooking for 2 minutes more. Pour in the corn, beans, tomatoes, and rice, stir to combine.

3. Fill each pepper equally with the beef mixture, top with cheese, and cook for 2-6 minutes or until the cheese is melted.

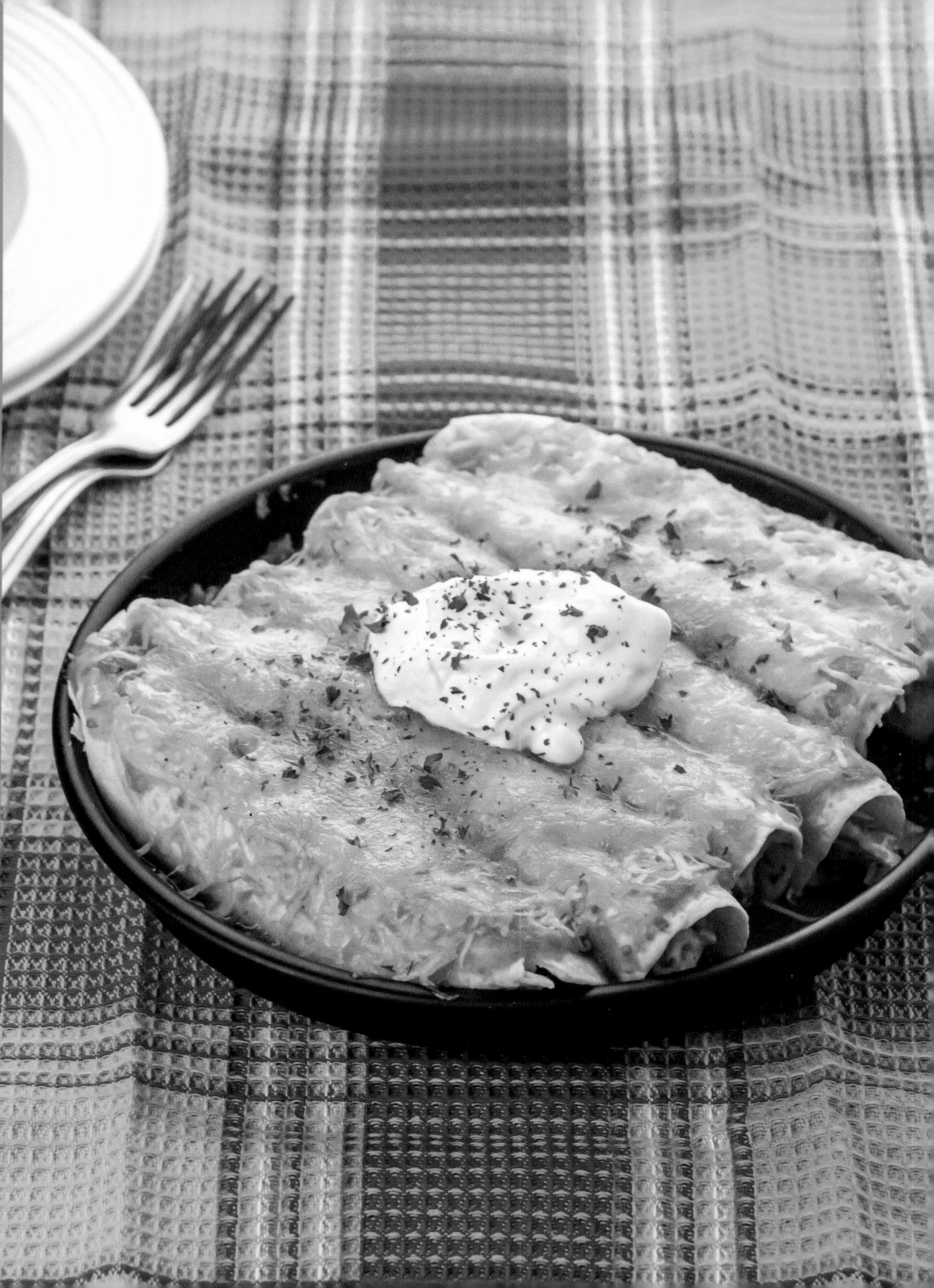

SALSA VERDE PORK ENCHILADAS

It's hard to resist the melty deliciousness of enchiladas, but when you're cooking for two, most recipes make enough to eat it for days! These pork enchiladas come together with minimal effort and are another double-duty recipe. First, by cooking the pork in your air fryer, then again to warm and melt the cheese on the enchiladas.

COOK TIME: 35 MIN | EFFORT: EASY

INGREDIENTS

- ½ teaspoon garlic powder
- 1 teaspoon chili powder
- ½ teaspoon paprika
- ½ teaspoon dried oregano
- ½ teaspoon ground cumin
- ¼ teaspoon salt
- ¼ teaspoon pepper
- 1 teaspoon canola oil
- 8 ounces (227 g) boneless pork shoulder
- 4 ounces (113 g) cream cheese, softened
- 1 (16-ounce [453 g]) jar salsa verde
- 6 (6-inch) tortillas
- 1 cup (83 g) shredded Mexican blend cheese
- Oil spray

DIRECTIONS

1. Preheat the air fryer to 380° F (190° C).

2. In a small bowl, combine the garlic powder, chili powder, paprika, oregano, cumin, salt, and pepper. Rub the pork with oil, then coat with the seasoning mixture.

3. Spray the air fryer with oil, add the pork, and cook for 18-22 minutes, flipping halfway through. Let rest for 10 minutes before shredding.

4. In a medium bowl, add the shredded pork and cream cheese, stirring until combined. Fill each tortilla evenly with the pork mixture, 1 tablespoon of salsa, and 2 tablespoons of cheese, rolling them closed.

5. Using a 6-inch baking pan, pour ¼ cup of the salsa on the bottom, add the rolled tortillas, and top with the remaining salsa and cheese. Tent with foil and cook for 6-10 minutes, removing the foil halfway through. Carefully remove the dish from the air fryer and let rest for 10 minutes before serving.

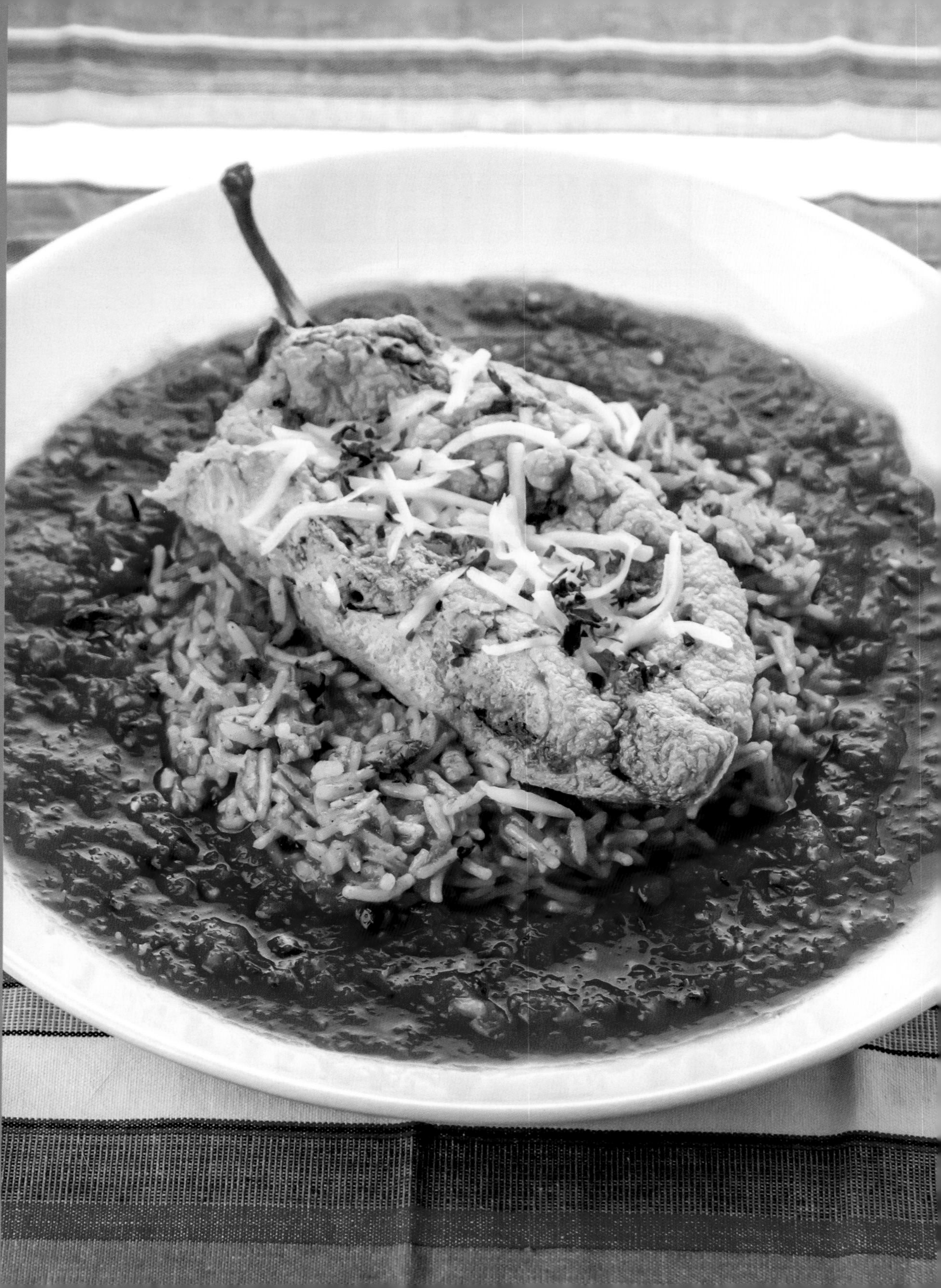

CHILE RELLENOS WITH SALSA ROJA

Deep-fried and stuffed with melted cheese, Chile Rellenos is a dish I can make over and over. The air fryer transforms this dish into a version that's just as good as its deep-fried sibling while being a lot healthier! And with only a few ingredients, you're just a few steps away from a delicious, mildly spicy dinner!

COOK TIME: 25 MIN | EFFORT: MODERATE

INGREDIENTS

- 2   large poblano peppers
- ½   cup (42 g) shredded Monterey Jack cheese
- 1   egg, separated
- 3   tablespoons (24 g) flour

SALSA

- 1   (8-ounce [227 g]) can stewed tomatoes with onion
- 5   sprigs cilantro
- 1   small jalapeño, stem and seeds removed, optional
- 1   garlic clove, minced

DIRECTIONS

1. Preheat the air fryer to 400° F (200° C). Add the poblanos to the air fryer and cook for 8-12 minutes, flipping halfway through, until the skins begin to blister. In a large bowl, add the peppers, cover with plastic wrap, and allow them to steam for 5 minutes. Carefully peel the skin off the peppers, slice a small opening into each pepper and remove the seeds. Carefully stuff each pepper with ¼ cup of cheese, and using toothpicks, seal closed. Set aside.

2. Reduce the air fryer to 380° F (190° C).

3. In a medium bowl, using an electric hand mixer on high speed, beat the egg white for 3-5 minutes, until stiff peaks form. Reduce the speed to low, add the yolk and mix until just combined. Lightly coat each pepper in flour, then dip and roll into the egg mixture. Line the air fryer with parchment paper and place each pepper into the air fryer. Cook for 8-12 minutes, or until lightly browned.

4. Meanwhile, in a blender, combine the stewed tomatoes, cilantro, jalapeño, and garlic until smooth. In a small saucepan over medium heat, add the salsa, and cook for 10 minutes, until heated through.

5. Serve the peppers with the salsa on the side or on top, with a side of spanish rice.

MANGIAMO!
(LET'S EAT)

While certainly not cooked in the traditional Italian fashion (sorry, nonna!), these Italian-inspired meals come together with little effort and sacrifice nothing when it comes to flavor. The air fryer gets you on the fast-track to dinner, and with classics like baked ziti, fried lasagna, chicken Parmesan, and more, I think even nonna would approve (but maybe don't tell her you made them in an air fryer...)

MOZZARELLA STUFFED CHICKEN MEATBALLS

When you can't decide between chicken Parmesan or spaghetti and meatballs, you no longer have to choose! You can have them both at the same time! I'm not sure anything is more satisfying than cutting into these cheese-filled meatballs. Serve them with a side of pasta, in a sub, or eat them on their own with a salad.

COOK TIME: 15 MIN | EFFORT: EASY

INGREDIENTS

- 8 ounces (227 g) pasta
- 8 ounces (227 g) ground chicken
- ½ teaspoon onion powder
- ½ teaspoon salt
- ¼ teaspoon pepper
- 1 egg
- ¼ cup (27 g) panko breadcrumbs
- 1 teaspoon dried basil
- ¼ cup (16 g) grated Parmesan cheese, plus extra for topping
- 2 ounces (142 g) mozzarella, cubed
- 1 cup (250 ml) marinara sauce

DIRECTIONS

1. Preheat the air fryer to 350° F (170° C).

2. Cook the pasta according to package directions and warm up the marinara.

3. Meanwhile, in a large bowl, using your hands, combine the chicken, onion powder, salt, pepper, egg, panko, basil, and Parmesan together. Divide the mixture into six, form into disks, place a mozzarella cube in the middle, and roll into a ball. Repeat. Spray the air fryer with oil, add the meatballs, and cook for 10-14 minutes, flipping halfway through.

4. Serve over pasta, topped with sauce and Parmesan.

ITALIAN SAUSAGE PASTA WITH TOMATO CREAM SAUCE

I've never had anything quite like this pasta, but in a way, it also felt very familiar because of its use of everyday ingredients. Its rich and creamy flavors pair so perfectly with the pronounced flavor of the Italian sausage. I could honestly eat it every day!

COOK TIME: 20 MIN | EFFORT: EASY

INGREDIENTS

- 8 ounces (227 g) sweet Italian sausage
- 1 medium onion, chopped
- 8 ounces (266 g) rotini pasta
- ½ cup (118 ml) heavy cream
- 2 tablespoons (22 g) tomato paste
- 1 teaspoon onion powder
- 1 teaspoon garlic powder
- 1 teaspoon Italian seasoning
- ½ teaspoon salt
- ¼ teaspoon pepper
- ¼ cup (16 g) grated Parmesan cheese, divided
- 1 handful spinach
- 1 cup (236 ml) pasta water, reserved
  Oil spray

DIRECTIONS

1. Preheat the air fryer to 360° F (180° C). Spray the air fryer with oil and add the sausage and onions. Cook for 16-20 minutes, turning the sausage and stirring the onions halfway through.

2. Bring a pot of water to a boil and cook the pasta according to package directions. Reserve 1 cup of pasta water before draining. Return the pasta to the pot.

3. Meanwhile, in a medium bowl, combine the cream, tomato paste, onion powder, garlic powder, Italian seasoning, salt, pepper, and 2 tablespoons of Parmesan. Pour the mixture into the pasta, add the spinach, cooked onion, and pasta water. Stir to combine. Divide into two serving bowls.

4. Slice the cooked sausages diagonally and place them on top of the pasta. Sprinkle with the remaining Parmesan and serve.

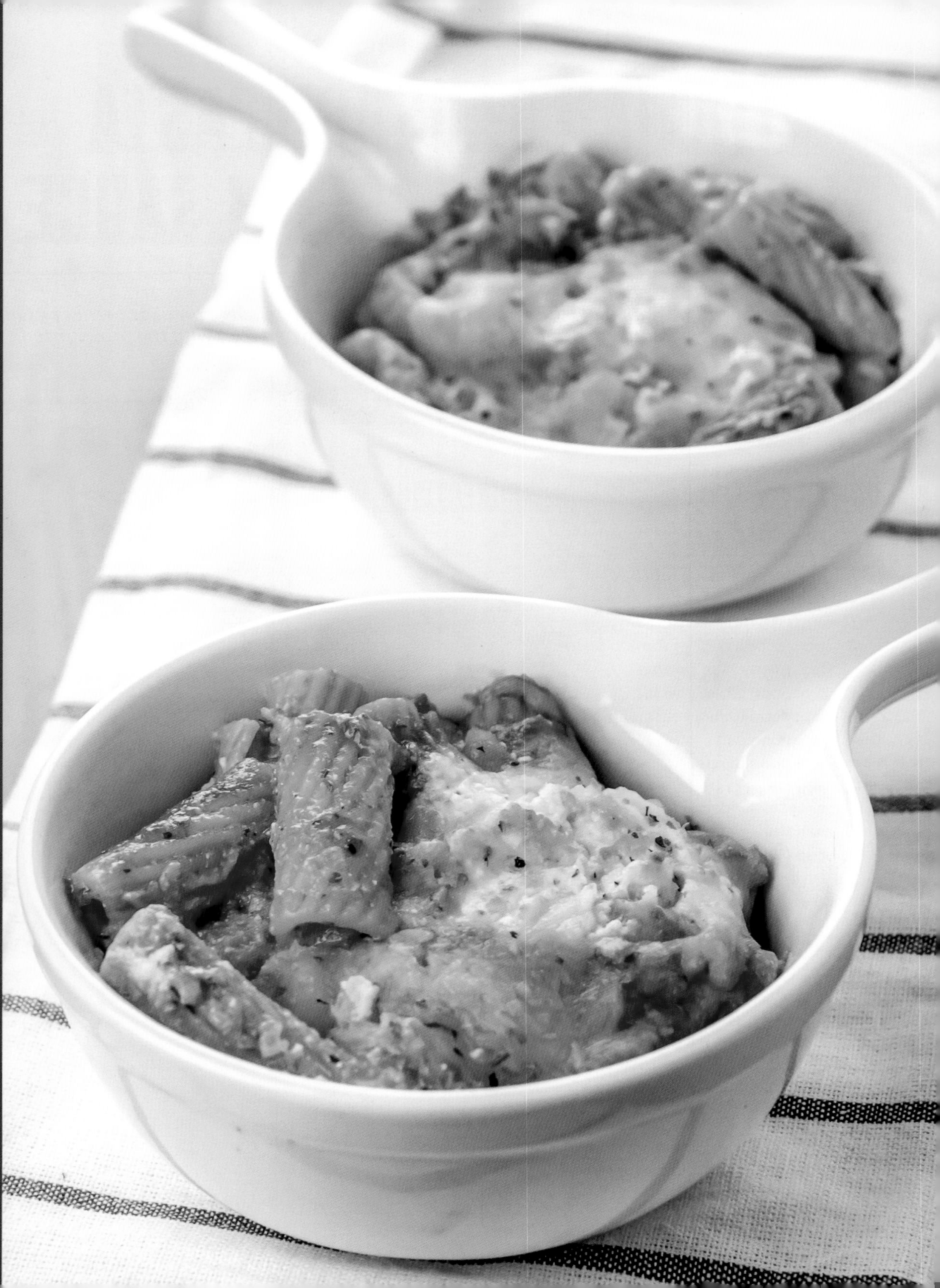

RICOTTA & MOZZARELLA BAKED ZITI

Who doesn't love a deliciously melty baked ziti? But turning on the oven for a small batch just doesn't always seem worth it. That's where the air fryer saves the day, yet again. You'll experience all of the satisfaction and won't have to heat up the whole house!

COOK TIME: 18 MIN | EFFORT: EASY

INGREDIENTS

- 8 ounces (119 g) rigatoni pasta
- ½ cup (123 g) ricotta cheese
- 1 tablespoon (15 ml) milk
- 1 tablespoon (6 g) grated Parmesan cheese
- ½ teaspoon salt
- ¼ teaspoon pepper
- ¼ teaspoon garlic powder
- ½ teaspoon onion powder
- ½ teaspoon Italian seasoning
- ¼ cup (28 g) shredded mozzarella cheese

SAUCE

- 1 (14-ounce [397 g]) can tomato sauce
- ½ teaspoon onion powder
- ½ teaspoon garlic powder
- 1 tablespoon (2 g) Italian seasoning
- ¼ teaspoon salt
- ⅛ teaspoon pepper

DIRECTIONS

1. Preheat the air fryer to 300° F (150° C).

2. Bring a pot of water to a boil and cook the pasta according to the package directions. Drain and set aside until ready to assemble.

3. Meanwhile, in a small bowl, stir together the ricotta, milk, Parmesan, salt, pepper, garlic powder, onion powder, and Italian seasoning. Set aside.

4. In a small saucepan over medium heat, combine the tomato sauce, onion powder, garlic powder, Italian seasoning, salt, and pepper. Bring to a simmer and reduce the heat to low, cooking for 5 minutes.

5. In a 6-inch baking dish, layer ½ cup of the sauce, the pasta, then dollop the ricotta mixture, pour over the remaining sauce, and top with the cheese. Cook for 4-8 minutes or until the cheese is melted and slightly browned. Scoop the ziti into two serving bowls and enjoy.

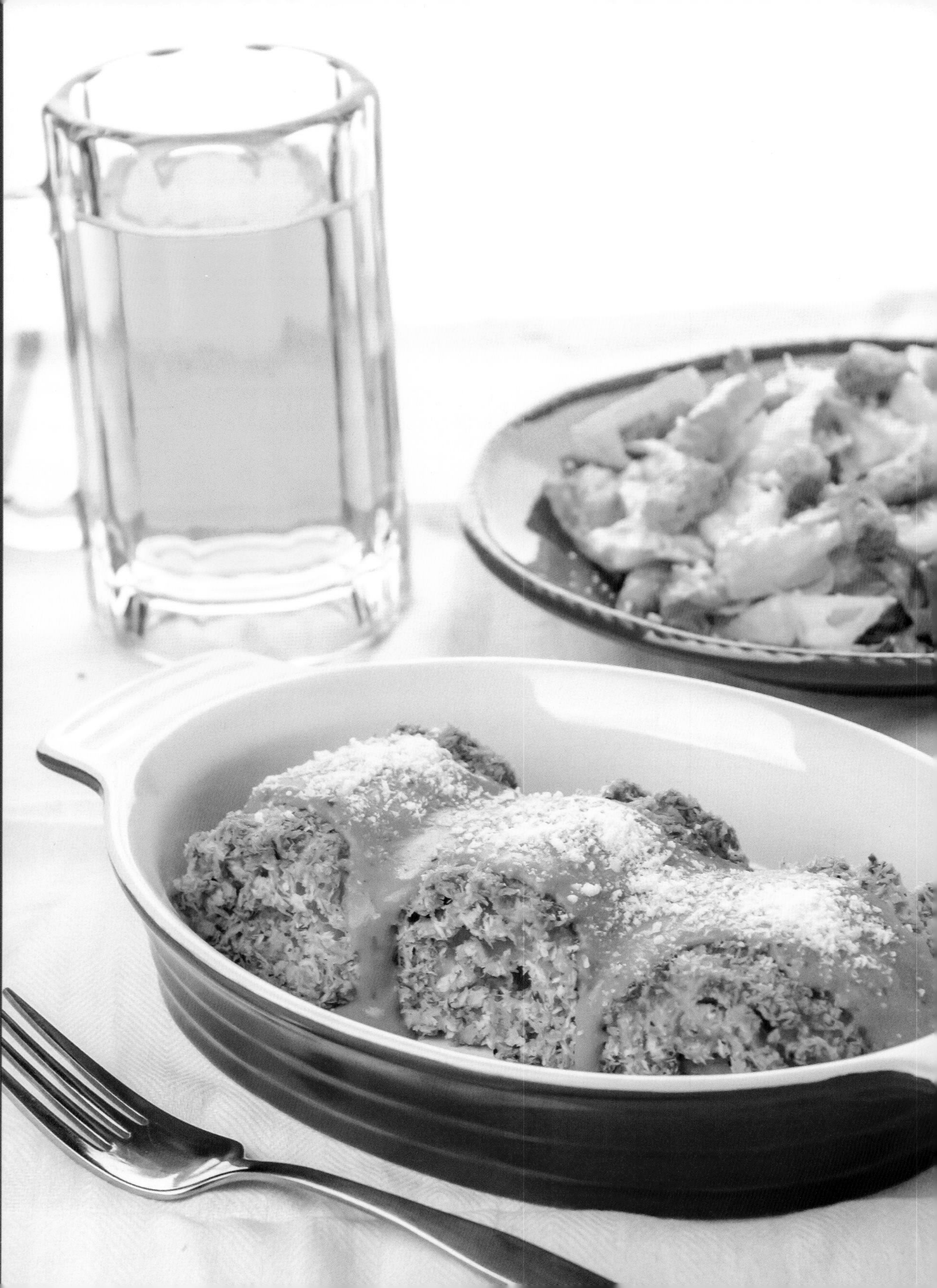

FRIED LASAGNA WITH CREAMY POMODORO SAUCE

Foods with textural contrasts are some of my favorite things to eat. This fried lasagna is a great example of this with its crispy exterior but smooth and creamy interior. A guilty pleasure becomes a little less guilty being made in the air fryer but tastes just as good as the original!

COOK TIME: 10 MIN | EFFORT: EASY

INGREDIENTS

- 1 cup (246 g) ricotta
- 2 tablespoons (12 g) grated Parmesan cheese
- ½ teaspoons salt
- ¼ teaspoon pepper
- 1 teaspoon Italian seasoning
- 1 tablespoon (8 g) flour
- 6 lasagna noodles, cooked, cooled, and ribbon edges removed
- 1 egg
- ½ cup (54 g) panko breadcrumbs
  Oil spray

SAUCE

- 2 tablespoons (28 g) butter
- 2 tablespoons (16 g) flour
- 1 cup (236 ml) milk
- ½ teaspoon garlic powder
- ½ teaspoon onion powder
- 1 teaspoon Italian seasoning
- 8 ounces (227 g) tomato sauce

DIRECTIONS

1. In a medium bowl, stir together the ricotta, Parmesan, salt, pepper, Italian seasoning, and flour. Spread 2 tablespoons of the ricotta mixture over the length of each noodle. Roll the filled noodles up and set them seam side down.

2. Preheat the air fryer to 400° F (200° C).

3. In a shallow bowl, beat the egg. In another shallow bowl, add the panko. Roll each lasagna roll in the egg and panko, pressing down lightly to ensure they stick. Add the rolls to the air fryer, spray with oil, and cook for 5-9 minutes, flipping and spraying halfway through.

4. Meanwhile, in a small saucepan over medium heat, melt the butter. Whisk in the flour, stirring continuously for 2 minutes. Gradually add in the milk, stirring after each addition. Add in the garlic powder, onion powder, and Italian seasoning. Pour in the tomato sauce, stir to combine, and cook for 4-5 minutes, until heated through.

5. Serve three lasagna rolls topped with the sauce.

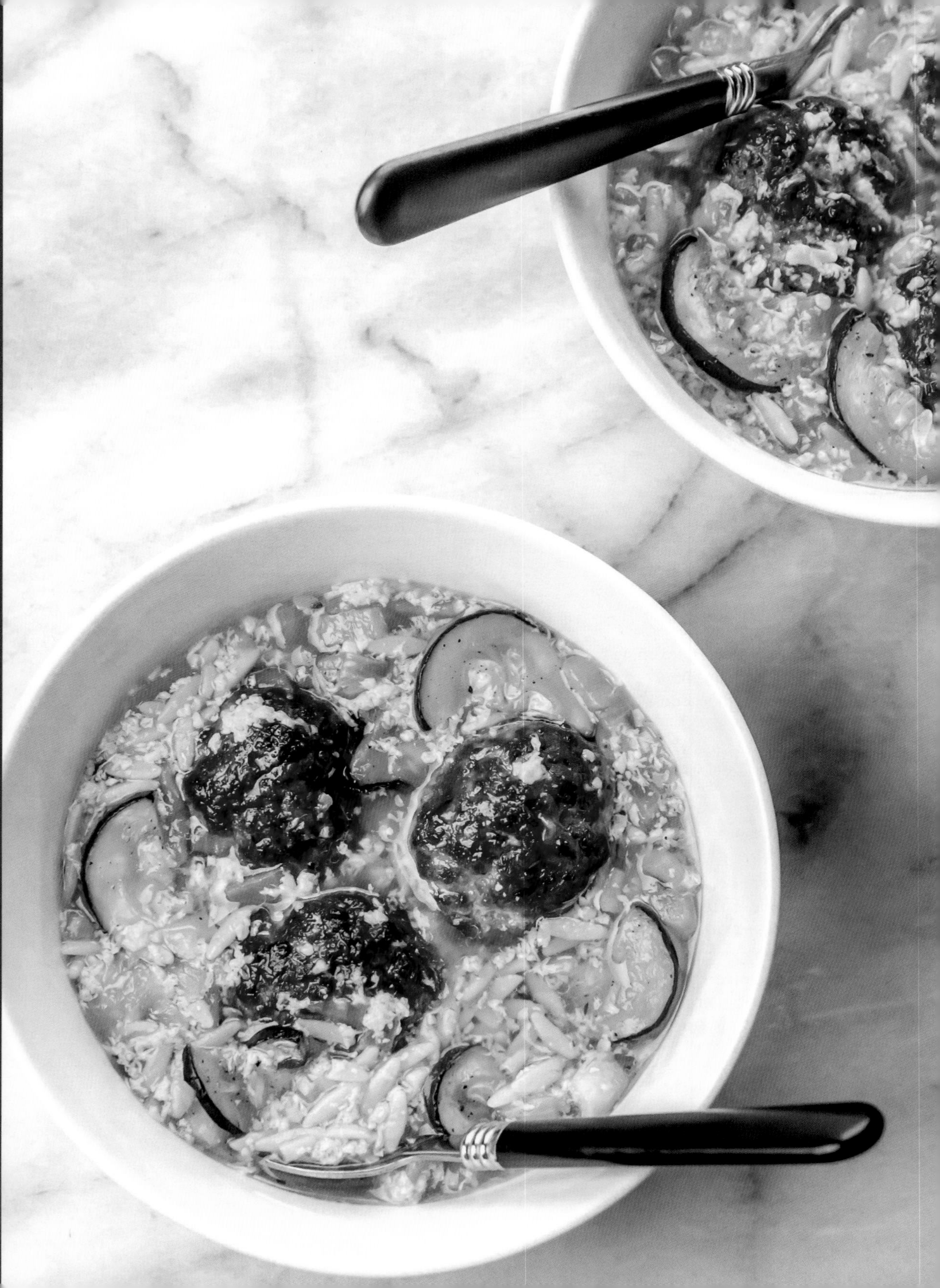

MEATBALL AND ORZO SOUP

Making soup in the air fryer sounds a little crazy but a quick glance at the steps reveals that the air fryer is used as an incredible shortcut for this delicious soup. Inspired by Italian wedding soup, but made it a lot more satisfying. By adding zucchini and making the meatballs larger, you have a soup worthy of being called a meal.

COOK TIME: 20 MIN | EFFORT: EASY

INGREDIENTS

- 8 ounces (227 g) ground beef
- ½ teaspoon Italian seasoning
- ½ teaspoon salt
- 1 garlic clove, minced
- 1 egg
- 3 tablespoons (18 g) grated Parmesan cheese
- 2 tablespoons (18 g) Italian seasoned breadcrumbs

BROTH

- 1 tablespoon (15 ml) canola oil
- 1 small onion, diced
- 1 garlic clove, minced
- 2 (14.5-ounce [444 ml]) cans chicken broth
- 1 zucchini, halved lengthwise and sliced
- ¼ cup (51 g) small pasta, such as orzo or acini di pepe

EGG MIX

- 1 egg
- 2 tablespoons (12 g) grated Parmesan cheese
- ⅛ teaspoon pepper

DIRECTIONS

1. Preheat the air fryer to 350° F (170° C).

2. In a large bowl, using your hands, combine the beef, Italian seasoning, salt, garlic, egg, Parmesan, and breadcrumbs. Divide into six and form into balls. Spray the air fryer with oil, add the meatballs, and cook for 6-10 minutes. Flip the meatballs and cook for 2 minutes more. Transfer to a plate, cover, and set aside.

3. Meanwhile, in a large saucepan over medium-high heat, warm the oil. Add the onion and garlic, cooking for 5 minutes, until translucent. Pour in the broth and bring to a boil, then add the zucchini and pasta. Reduce the heat to low, cover, and simmer for 10 minutes. Add the meatballs and cook 5 minutes more.

4. In a small bowl, stir together the egg, Parmesan, and pepper. Stir the soup in one direction, slowly pouring in the egg mixture. Divide into two bowls and serve.

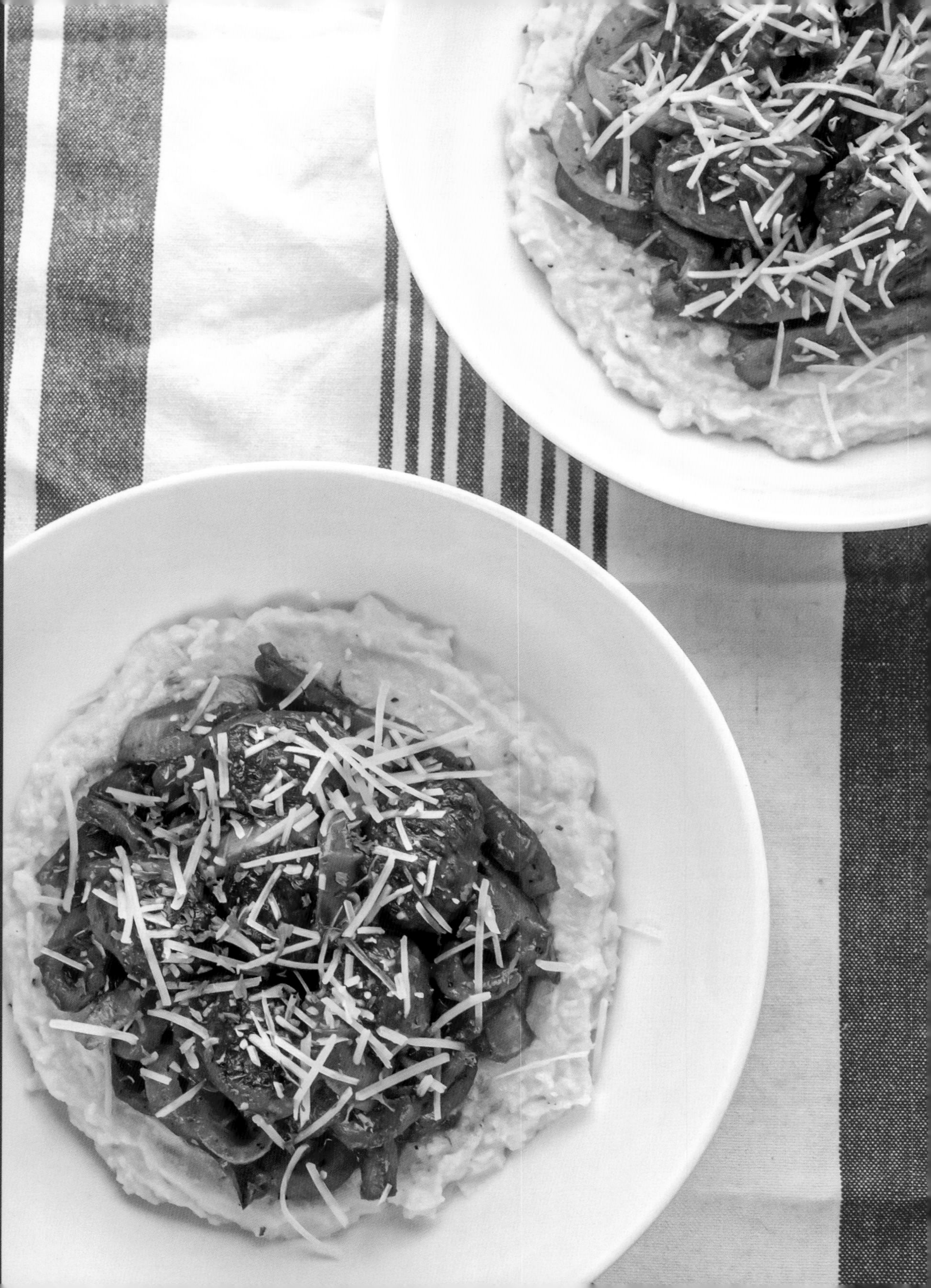

SAUSAGE MEATBALLS WITH CREAMY POLENTA

I don't often eat polenta but every time I have it, I wonder why I don't make it more often. It comes together easily, it's affordable, and can be very delicious. In this recipe, Italian sausage meatballs with roasted peppers and onions are mixed with a rich, wine-infused tomato sauce. Served over polenta, this meal brings a unique contrast of both flavor and texture.

COOK TIME: 30 MIN | EFFORT: EASY

INGREDIENTS

- 8 ounces (227 g) ground Italian sausage
- 1 medium onion, sliced
- 1 medium green pepper, sliced
- 3 tablespoons (33 g) tomato paste
- ½ cup (118 ml) vermouth or white wine
- ½ cup (118 ml) chicken broth
- 1 teaspoon Italian seasoning
- ½ teaspoon garlic powder
- ½ teaspoon salt
- ¼ teaspoon pepper

POLENTA

- 1 cup (236 ml) chicken broth
- 1 cup (236 ml) milk
- ½ cup (118 ml) yellow cornmeal
- 2 tablespoons (12 g) shredded Parmesan cheese, plus more for serving

DIRECTIONS

1. Preheat the air fryer to 360° F (180° C). Using your hands, divide the Italian sausage into 12 equally-sized meatballs. Add the onions, peppers, and meatballs to the air fryer, spray with oil, and cook for 16-20 minutes, stirring halfway through.

2. Meanwhile, in a small bowl, combine the tomato paste, vermouth, broth, Italian seasoning, garlic powder, salt, and pepper.

3. In a medium saucepan over medium heat, pour in the broth and milk. Bring the mixture to a boil and gradually stir in the cornmeal. Cook for 5 minutes, or until it no longer looks wet. Stir in the Parmesan and continue stirring until melted. Divide into two serving bowls, and set aside.

4. In a small pan over medium heat, pour in the sauce, meatballs, onions, and peppers. Bring to a simmer and continue cooking for about 5 minutes, until the mixture thickens and has slightly reduced.

5. Pour the sausage mixture evenly over each bowl of polenta and serve topped with more Parmesan cheese.

SUPREME PIZZA STUFFED CALZONES

I love pizza but thinking about cleaning all of the loose cheese at the bottom of the air fryer sounded like more hassle than it's worth. Then it hit me, why not try a calzone? After all, it's basically an enclosed pizza! So I tried one of my favorite pizzas in a calzone and the rest is history.

COOK TIME: 12 MIN | EFFORT: MODERATE

DOUGH

- ¾ cup (177 ml) warm water
- 1 tablespoon (12 g) sugar
- 1 packet (2¼ teaspoons [6 g]) active dry yeast
- 2 tablespoons (30 ml) canola oil
- 1 teaspoon salt
- 2 cups (240 g) flour

INGREDIENTS

- 1 tablespoon (15 ml) canola oil
- 1 small onion, diced
- 1 small green pepper, diced
- ½ cup (118 ml) pizza sauce, plus extra for dipping
- 1 (2.25-ounce [64 g]) can sliced black olives, drained
- 1 (4-ounce [113 g]) can sliced mushrooms, drained
- 20 pepperoni slices
- 1 cup (112 g) shredded mozzarella cheese
- 1 egg mixed with 1 tablespoon (15 ml) water
- 2 tablespoons (12 g) shredded Parmesan cheese, optional

DIRECTIONS

1. In a medium bowl, combine the water, sugar, and yeast. Allow the mixture to sit for 5 minutes; once foamy and fragrant, add the oil, salt, and flour. Stir the mixture until a dough forms. Transfer the dough to a clean, greased bowl. Cover with plastic wrap and allow to rise for 1 hour or until doubled in size.

2. Preheat the air fryer to 350° F (170° C). Add the onions and peppers to the air fryer, spray with oil, and cook for 6-10 minutes, stirring halfway through.

3. Transfer the dough to a floured surface and knead a few times. Cut the dough in half and using a rolling pin, shape each one into a 12-inch circle, about ¼-inch thick. On half of each circle, spread ¼ cup of pizza sauce, half of the onion and pepper mixture, half of the olives, half of the mushrooms, 10 pepperoni, and ½ cup of the cheese. Fold the circle closed and crimp the edges.

4. Brush the dough with the egg mixture and optionally top with Parmesan.

5. Carefully line the air fryer with parchment paper and add the calzones, cooking one at a time, for 15 minutes, until crispy and a light golden color. Serve with a side of pizza sauce for dipping.

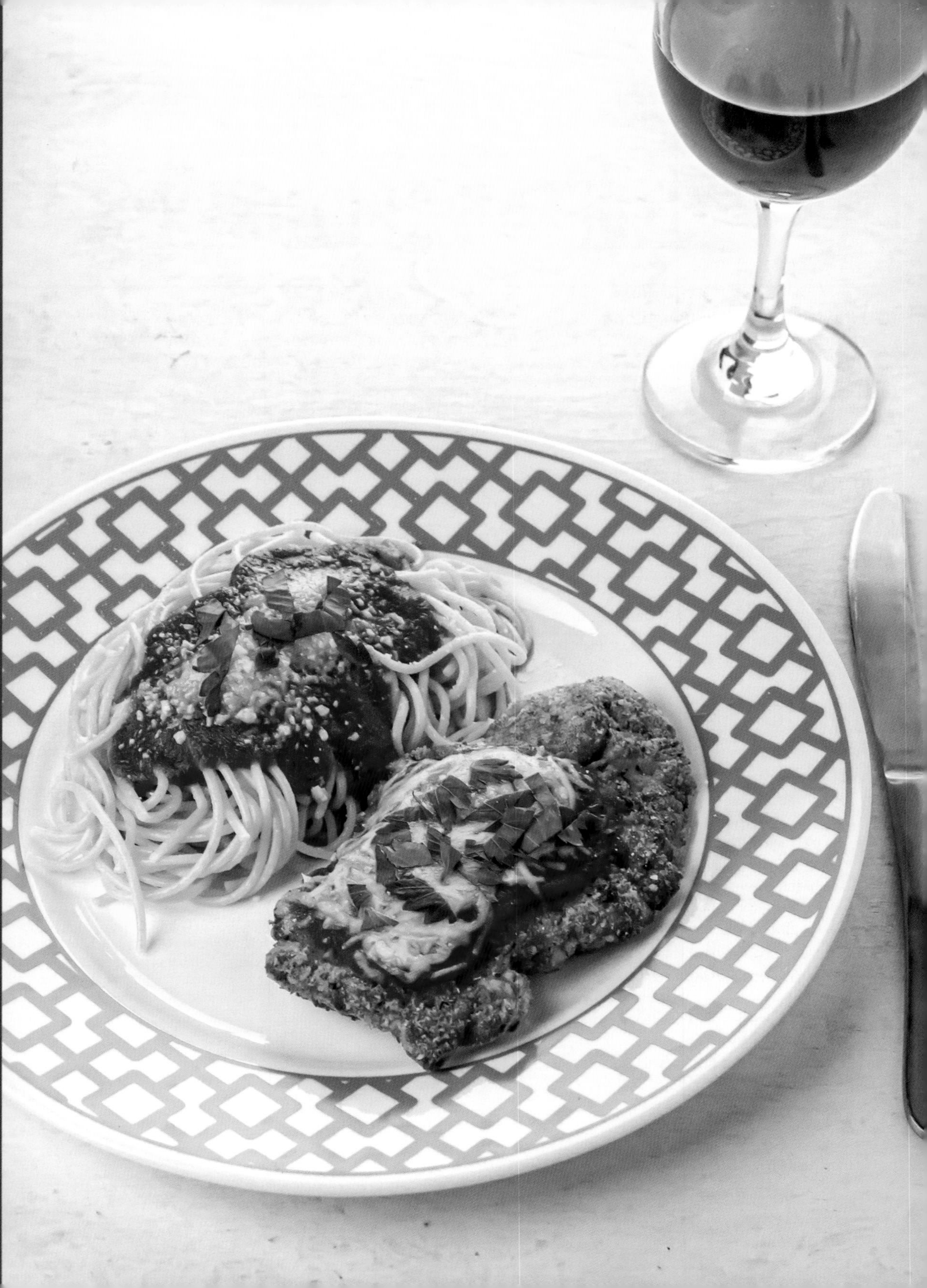

CLASSIC CHICKEN PARMESAN

Chicken Parmesan may be one of the most popular dishes ordered at an Italian restaurant, so why not be able to make this classic at home in your air fryer? This recipe is simple, quick, delicious, and healthier! The only difficult thing will be deciding what you're going to order at the Italian restaurant from now on.

COOK TIME: 15 MIN | EFFORT: EASY

INGREDIENTS

- ¼ cup (32 g) flour
- ¼ teaspoon salt
- ⅛ teaspoon pepper
- 1 egg
- ¼ cup (36 g) Italian breadcrumbs
- 2 tablespoons (12 g) grated Parmesan cheese
- 4 boneless, skinless chicken thighs
- 8 ounces (227 g) spaghetti noodles
- ½ cup (56 g) shredded mozzarella

SAUCE

- 1 (14-ounce [400 g]) can tomato sauce
- 1 tablespoon (2 g) Italian seasoning
- ¼ teaspoon salt
- ⅛ teaspoon pepper
- ½ teaspoon onion powder
- ½ teaspoon garlic powder

DIRECTIONS

1. Preheat the air fryer to 380° F (190° C).

2. In a resealable bag, combine the flour, salt, and pepper. In a shallow bowl, beat the egg. In a small bowl, stir together the breadcrumbs and Parmesan.

3. Add the chicken to the flour mixture and shake to coat. Dip each chicken in the egg, and then breadcrumb mixture, pressing down lightly to ensure they stick. Spray the air fryer with oil, add the chicken, spray with oil, and cook for 8-12 minutes, flipping halfway through, until crispy and a light golden color.

4. Bring a pot of water to a boil, add the spaghetti, and cook according to the package directions. Drain and set aside.

5. Meanwhile, in a small saucepan over medium heat, stir together the tomato sauce, Italian seasoning, salt, pepper, onion powder, and garlic powder. Bring to a simmer, reduce heat to low, and cook for 8-10 minutes; stirring continuously.

6. Spoon 1 tablespoon of sauce on each piece of chicken, top with 2 tablespoons of cheese, and cook for 2 minutes, until the cheese is melted. Serve with a side of spaghetti.

TAKEOUT
AT HOME

Would you believe me if I said you can recreate some of your favorite Asian-inspired meals in your own kitchen but without having to use a wok? Well, you may think I sound crazy, but it can be done and even better, it can be done with your air fryer! Once you give these recipes a try, you will be crazy about cooking your favorite takeout meals right at home, too!

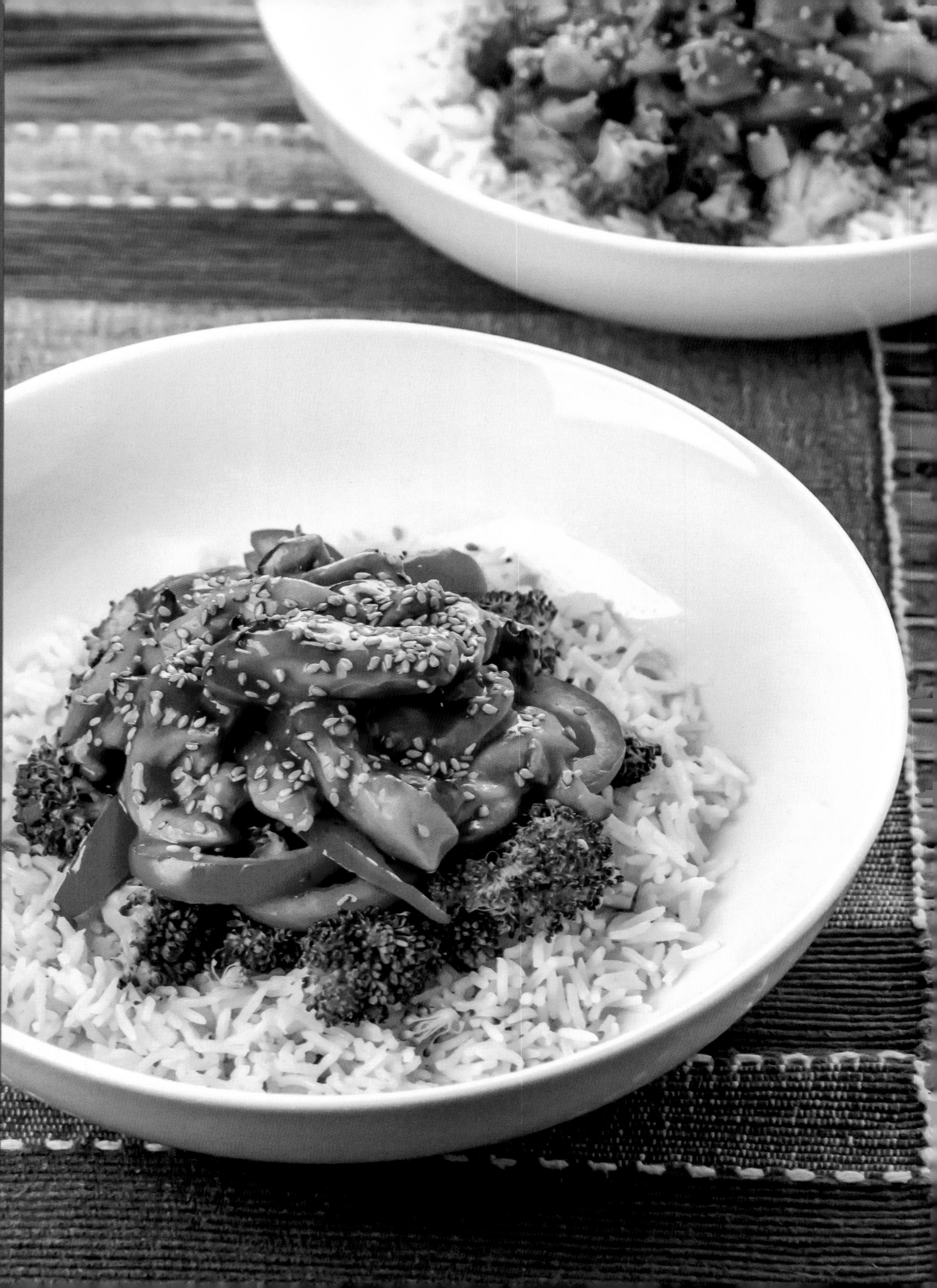

CHICKEN & VEGETABLE STIR FRY

Chicken stir fry is delicious and with all those vegetables, you'd think it's a nice, healthy choice for dinner. As good intentioned as it may be, stir fry is often soaked in oil. But not when you make it in your air fryer! This stir fry (or faux fry as I call it) is not only healthier, it's easier too, all while delivering on the same great flavor!

COOK TIME: 12 MIN | EFFORT: EASY

INGREDIENTS

- ¼ cup (60 ml) low-sodium soy sauce
- ½ cup (118 ml) chicken broth
- 2 teaspoons (6 g) cornstarch mixed with 2 teaspoons (10 ml) water
- 2 teaspoons (10 ml) honey
- 1 teaspoon rice wine vinegar
- ½ teaspoons powdered ginger
- 1 garlic cloves, minced
- 8 ounces (227 g) boneless skinless chicken thighs, cut into bite-sized pieces
- 1 cup (195g) uncooked rice
- 1 small head broccoli, cut into ¼-inch pieces and florets
- 1 small red pepper, sliced

DIRECTIONS

1. In a medium bowl, stir together the soy sauce, broth, cornstarch mixture, honey, vinegar, ginger, and garlic. Add the chicken and marinate for 1 hour.

2. In a small saucepan, cook the rice according to the package directions.

3. Preheat the air fryer to 390° F (190° C). Spray the air fryer with oil, add the chicken, broccoli, and peppers, and spray with oil. Cook for 8-12 minutes, stirring halfway through.

4. Meanwhile, in a small saucepan over medium-low heat, add the marinade and bring to a simmer, cooking about 6 minutes until it becomes a sauce. Add the chicken mixture into the sauce, stirring to coat. Serve over rice, and optionally top with sesame seed.

CHICKEN TERIYAKI WITH BOK CHOY

Chicken teriyaki is no doubt a famous takeout meal, but have you ever made it from scratch? It comes together with minimal effort and is made healthier, thanks to the air fryer! Served with crunchy bok choy, dinner is ready in minutes!

COOK TIME: 12 MIN | EFFORT: EASY

INGREDIENTS

- 8   ounces (227 g) boneless skinless chicken thighs, cut into bite-sized pieces
- ½   teaspoon salt
- ⅛   teaspoon pepper
- 1   baby bok choy, halved
- 1   cup (195 g) uncooked rice
     Oil spray

SAUCE

- ¼   cup (59 ml) low-sodium soy sauce
- 2   tablespoons (30 ml) honey
- 2   tablespoons (30 ml) dry sherry
- 2   tablespoons (30 ml) rice wine vinegar
- 1   tablespoon (9 g) cornstarch mixed with 1 tablespoon (15 ml) water
- ½   teaspoon toasted sesame oil
- ¼   teaspoon powdered ginger
- 2   garlic cloves, minced
     Sesame seeds, for topping
     Green onions, sliced, optional for topping

DIRECTIONS

1. Preheat the air fryer to 360° F (180° C).

2. Season the chicken with salt and pepper, spray the air fryer with oil, and add the chicken. Cook for 10-14 minutes, stirring and adding the bok choy halfway through.

3. In a small saucepan, cook the rice according to the package directions.

4. Meanwhile, in a small saucepan over medium heat, add the soy sauce, honey, sherry, vinegar, cornstarch mixture, sesame oil, ginger, and garlic. Bring to a boil and cook for 6 minutes, until thickened. Add the chicken to the pan, stirring to coat. Serve over rice, with the bok choy on the side and optionally topped with sesame seeds and green onion.

KOREAN BEEF AND BROCCOLI

This is a quick and easy way to make BBQ Korean beef, no wok required! Because the broccoli, onion, and beef roast in the air fryer, that little bit of char from the roasting adds a whole extra layer of flavor. Tossed in a sweet and slightly spicy sauce, I can tell you that it does not get any easier than this!

COOK TIME: 20 MIN | EFFORT: EASY

INGREDIENTS

- 2 cups (142 g) broccoli florets
- 1 medium onion, sliced
- 8 ounces (227 g) skirt steak, fat trimmed off, cut into 1-inch chunks
- 1 cup (195 g) uncooked rice
- 2 tablespoons (27 g) brown sugar
- ¼ cup (59 ml) beef broth
- 3 tablespoons (44 ml) low-sodium soy sauce
- 1 tablespoon (15 ml) toasted sesame oil
- 1 teaspoon sriracha
- ½ teaspoon powdered ginger
- 1 teaspoon vinegar
- 2 garlic cloves, minced

DIRECTIONS

1. Preheat the air fryer to 400° F (200° C).

2. Spray the air fryer with oil, add the broccoli and onions, and cook for 10-14 minutes. Stir and add the beef, cooking for 4-8 minutes more.

3. Meanwhile, in a small saucepan, cook rice according to the package directions.

4. In a medium saucepan over medium heat, add the brown sugar, broth, soy sauce, sesame oil, sriracha, ginger, vinegar, and garlic, stirring to combine and bring to a simmer. Add the beef and onions to the sauce, stirring to coat.

5. Serve the beef and broccoli over rice.

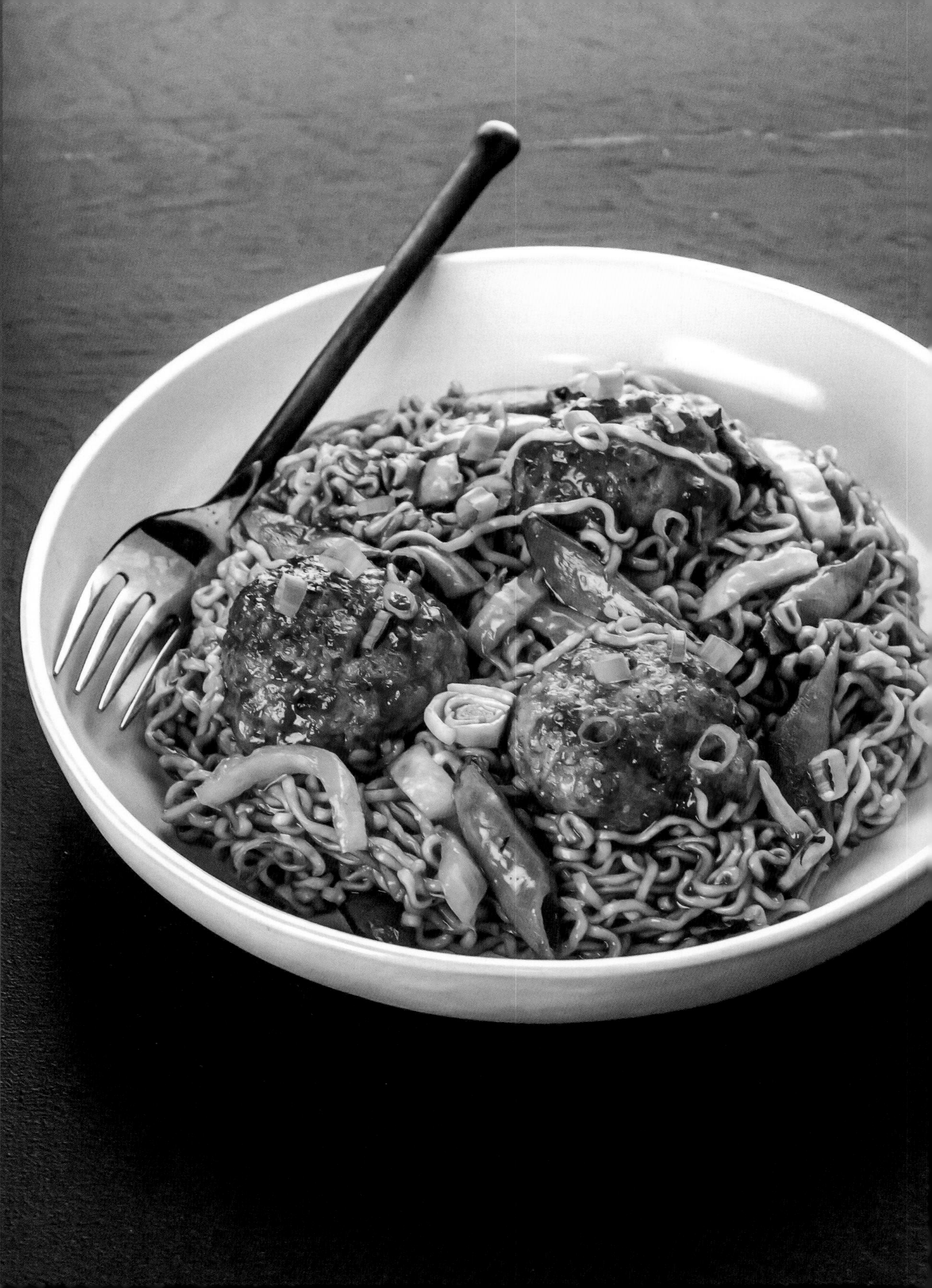

BOURBON PORK MEATBALL RAMEN

These are not your standard meatballs! Turn ground pork into these tender and juicy meatballs with a bit of an Asian flair. Served on top of upgraded ramen noodles and a bourbon sauce, this dish will be turning up the flavor on tonight's dinner.

COOK TIME: 25 MIN | EFFORT: EASY

INGREDIENTS

- 8 ounces (227 g) ground pork
- ½ teaspoon salt
- ¼ teaspoon pepper
- 1 garlic clove, minced
- 2 tablespoons (30 ml) sweet chili sauce
- 1 egg
- ¼ cup (27 g) panko breadcrumbs
- 1 baby bok choy, chopped
- 1½ cups (147 g) sliced snap peas
- 2 packages ramen, discard flavor packets

SAUCE

- ¼ cup (59 ml) bourbon whiskey
- ¼ cup (59 ml) honey
- ¼ cup (59 ml) water
- 1 garlic clove, minced
- ¼ cup (59 ml) low-sodium soy sauce
- 2 tablespoons (30 ml) apple cider vinegar
- ⅛ teaspoon pepper
- ¼ teaspoon powdered ginger
- 1 tablespoon (9 g) cornstarch mixed with 1 tablespoon (15 ml) water

DIRECTIONS

1. Preheat the air fryer to 350° F (170° C).

2. In a medium bowl, using your hands, combine the pork, salt, pepper, garlic, chili sauce, egg, and panko, until just incorporated, and form into six even meatballs. Spray the air fryer with oil, add the meatballs, and cook for 6-10 minutes. Flip the meatballs, add the bok choy and snap peas, and continue cooking for another 4-6 minutes.

3. Meanwhile, in a large pot, cook the ramen according to package directions, reserving ½ cup of pasta water before draining, then return the noodles to the pot; set aside.

4. In a medium saucepan over medium heat, add the bourbon, honey, water, garlic, soy sauce, vinegar, pepper, and ginger, cook for 5-7 minutes, until reduced by half. Add in the cornstarch mixture, stirring until thickened. In the pot with the noodles, add the meatballs, snap peas, bok choy, sauce, and pasta water, tossing until everything is well coated. Serve with three meatballs per bowl.

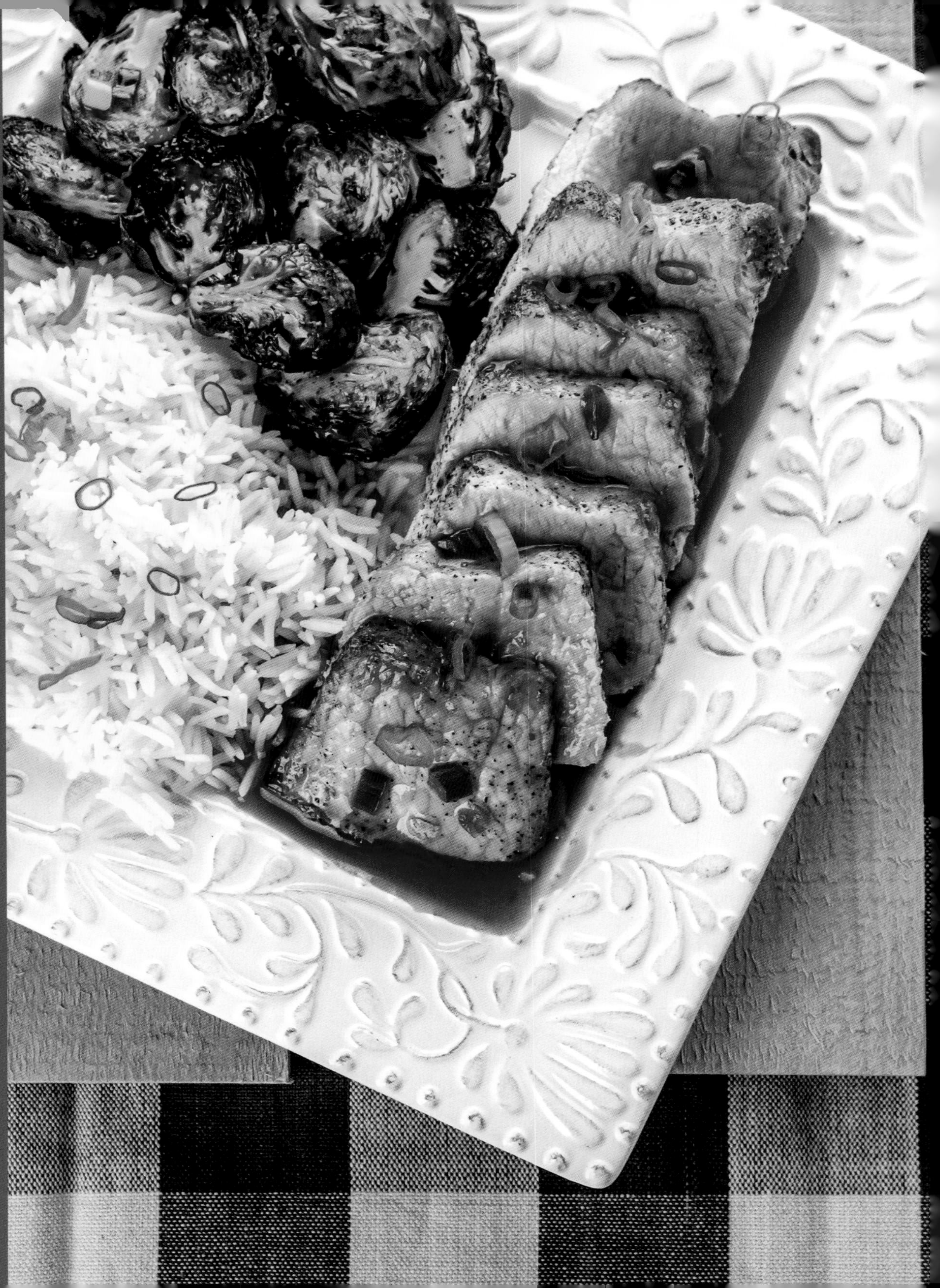

SWEET CHILI PORK WITH BRUSSELS SPROUTS

If you haven't made pork tenderloin in the air fryer, this is a recipe you have to try! The best part is the pork and Brussels cook together, making the most of your time. That gives you a few moments to make the sweet Asian sauce. Served with rice, you have a full meal in minutes!

COOK TIME: 15 MIN | EFFORT: EASY

INGREDIENTS

- 1 cup (195 g) uncooked rice
- 8 ounces (227 g) pork tenderloin
- 1 teaspoon salt, divided
- ½ teaspoon pepper, divided
- 8 ounces (227 g) Brussels sprouts, quartered
- 1 teaspoon oil
  Oil spray

SAUCE

- 3 tablespoons (44 g) low-sodium soy sauce
- 1 tablespoon (15 ml) sweet chili sauce
- 1 teaspoon toasted sesame oil
- 1 teaspoon honey
- ½ teaspoon rice wine vinegar
  Sriracha, to taste
- 1 green onion, sliced
- 2 teaspoons (6 g) cornstarch mixed with 2 teaspoons (10 ml) water

DIRECTIONS

1. Preheat the air fryer to 400° F (200° C).

2. In a medium pot, cook the rice according to the package directions.

3. Meanwhile, season the pork tenderloin with half of the salt and pepper, spray the air fryer with the oil, add the tenderloin, and cook for 6-10 minutes.

4. Meanwhile, in a medium bowl, add the Brussels sprouts, oil, remaining salt, and pepper, tossing to coat. Add the Brussels to the air fryer and continue cooking for another 10-14 minutes. Let the tenderloin rest for 5 minutes before slicing and serving.

5. In a small saucepan over medium-low heat, combine the soy sauce, sweet chili sauce, sesame oil, honey, vinegar, and sriracha, and bring to a simmer. Add in the green onion and cornstarch mixture, stirring until thickened.

6. Serve the pork sliced, topped with the sauce alongside the roasted brussels sprouts and rice.

MONGOLIAN BEEF WITH MUSHROOMS

Hopefully, you've caught on to how amazing the air fryer is at making healthier versions of our takeout favorites. This Mongolian Beef is no exception with its seasoned beef, and tender mushrooms slathered in a deliciously savory sauce. One bite and you'll be hooked!

COOK TIME: 10 MIN | EFFORT: EASY

INGREDIENTS

- 1 cup (195 g) uncooked rice
- 8 ounces (227 g) skirt steak, just into bite-sized pieces
- ½ teaspoon salt
- ¼ teaspoon pepper
- 2 tablespoons (17 g) cornstarch
- 8 ounces (227 g) button mushrooms, quartered
- Oil spray

SAUCE

- ¼ cup (59 ml) water
- ½ teaspoon toasted sesame oil
- 1 garlic clove, minced
- 2 tablespoons (27 g) brown sugar
- 2 tablespoons (30 ml) low-sodium soy sauce
- ⅛ teaspoon powdered ginger
- 1 teaspoon rice wine vinegar
- ¼ teaspoon Sriracha, optional
- 1 green onion, sliced, for serving

DIRECTIONS

1. Preheat the air fryer to 360° F (180° C).

2. In a medium pot, cook the rice according to the package directions.

3. Season the steak with salt and pepper. In a resealable bag, add the cornstarch and steak; shaking to coat. Spray the air fryer with oil, add the beef and mushrooms, and spray with oil until fully coated. Cook for 6-10 minutes, stirring and spraying with oil halfway through.

4. Meanwhile, in a medium saucepan over medium heat, stir together the water, sesame oil, garlic, brown sugar, soy sauce, ginger, vinegar, and sriracha. Add the beef and mushrooms to the sauce and cook for 2-3 minutes, stirring until coated. Serve over rice and top with green onion.

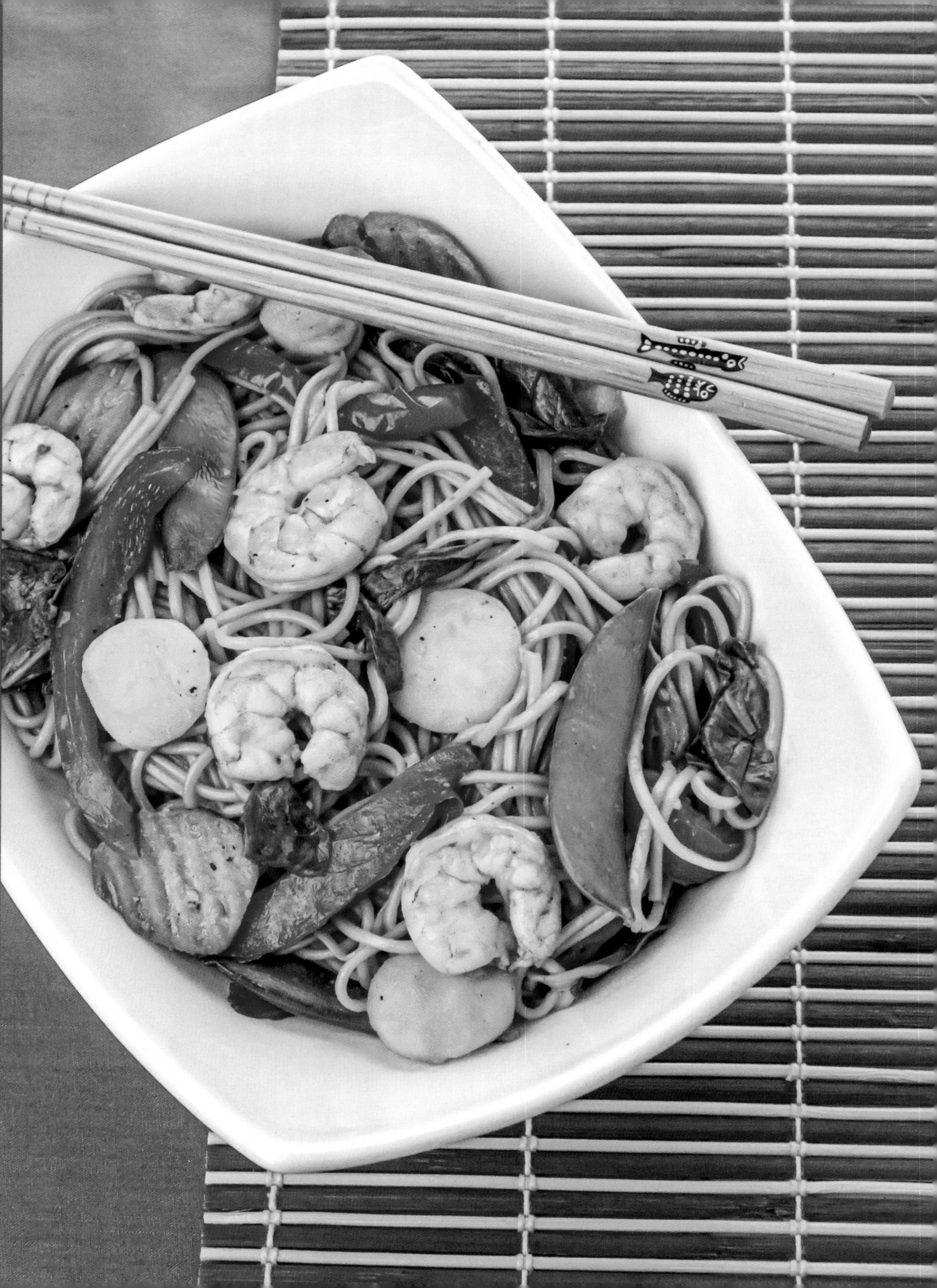

SHRIMP & VEGETABLE LO MEIN

When I wrote the outline for this cookbook, I had this shrimp lo mein on the list. The looks I got would make you think I was crazy but I knew I could make it work, the method just needed a little reworking to accommodate the air fryer. Sure enough, I was right, and here it is folks, shrimp lo mein!

COOK TIME: 25 MIN | EFFORT: EASY

INGREDIENTS

- 1   small carrot, sliced
- 1   red pepper, thinly sliced
- ½   cup (62 g) sliced water chestnuts
- ½   cup (49 g) snap peas
- 8   ounces (227 g) shrimp, peeled, deveined, and tails removed
- 8   ounces (227 g) lo mein egg noodles
- 3   cups (90 g) baby spinach

SAUCE

- 1   tablespoon (15 ml) low-sodium soy sauce, or more, to taste
- 2   teaspoons (8 g) sugar
- 1   teaspoon toasted sesame oil
- ½   teaspoon powdered ginger
- 2   garlic cloves, minced
- ½   teaspoon Sriracha, or more, to taste

DIRECTIONS

1. Preheat the air fryer to 400° F (200° C).

2. Spray the air fryer with oil, add the carrots and cook for 4-8 minutes. Add the peppers and cook for 4-8 minutes, then add the water chestnuts, peas, and shrimp, continuing to cook for 4-8 minutes more.

3. Meanwhile, bring a pot of water to a boil and cook the noodles according to package directions; drain and return to the pot.

4. In a small bowl, whisk together the soy sauce, sugar, sesame oil, ginger, garlic, and Sriracha; set aside.

5. Add the shrimp, vegetables, spinach, and sauce mixture to the noodles. Stir to combine, and serve.

AMERICAN
CLASSICS

While looking through this chapter, you may feel it's a bit random; some of the recipes are comfort foods like roast beef and country fried pork, while things like steak salads and chicken cordon bleu are different but still well known. What's the connection? While maybe not all of them originate from the USA, many of these dishes have impacted or changed the way we eat here in America. This chapter celebrates those foods!

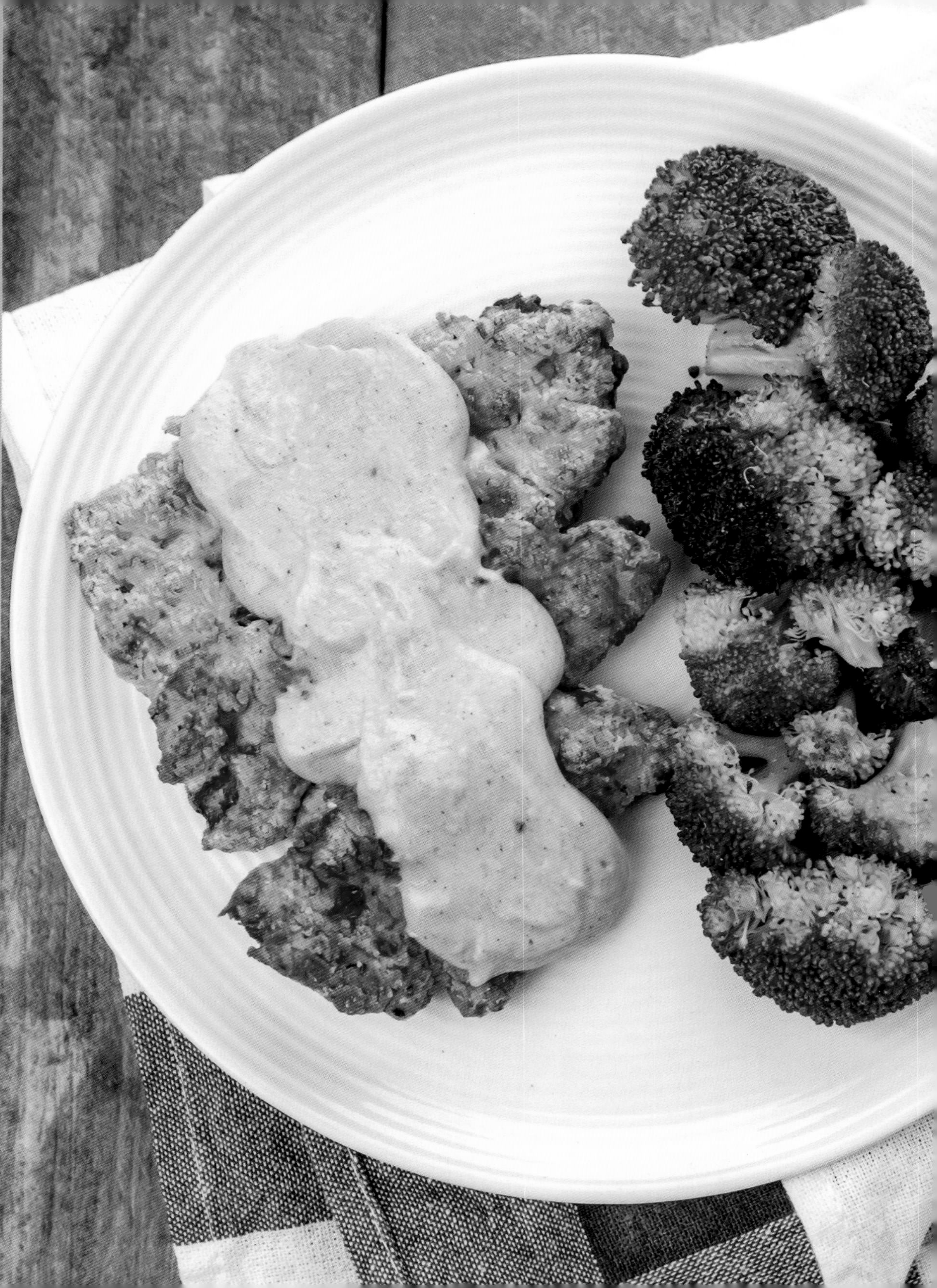

COUNTRY FRIED PORK CUTLETS

A mashup of country fried steak and breaded pork chops, I bring you, country fried pork! Made with tenderloin that's sliced into medallions and breaded in a fried chicken coating. It's only made better being topped with country gravy! Serve it alongside your favorite vegetable and dinner is ready!

COOK TIME: 16 MIN | EFFORT: EASY

INGREDIENTS

- 8 ounces (227 g) pork tenderloin, cut into 1-inch thick slices
- 1 teaspoon salt
- 1 teaspoon pepper
- 1 teaspoon garlic powder
- 1 teaspoon paprika
- ½ teaspoon onion powder
- ½ teaspoon Italian seasoning
- ⅓ cup (43g) flour
- 2 tablespoons (15g) cornstarch
- ½ teaspoon baking powder
- 2 eggs

GRAVY

- 1 tablespoon (14g) butter
- 1 tablespoon (8 g) flour
- ½ cup (118 ml) milk, warmed
- ½ teaspoon salt
- ½ teaspoon pepper

DIRECTIONS

1. Using the palm of your hand, press the pork into thin cutlets, about a ¼-inch thick.

2. In a small bowl, combine the salt, pepper, garlic powder, paprika, onion powder, and Italian seasoning. Season the pork on both sides with half of the spice mixture and set aside.

3. In a large resealable bag, mix together the flour, cornstarch, baking powder, and the remaining spice mix. In a medium bowl, beat the eggs. Place the pork in the flour mixture and shake until fully coated. Dip the pork into the eggs, then return to the flour mixture. Transfer the pork to a plate and allow it to rest for 15 minutes.

4. Preheat the air fryer to 400° F (200° C). Spray the air fryer with oil, add the pork, spray with oil, and cook for 12-16 minutes, flipping halfway through, and spraying with oil.

5. Meanwhile, in a medium saucepan over medium heat, melt the butter. Add the flour, stirring continuously, about 2 minutes, until the flour starts to resemble the color of peanut butter. Gradually pour in the milk, stirring after each addition. Once the mixture begins to thicken, reduce the heat to low and stir in the salt and pepper.

6. Serve the pork topped with the country gravy and your choice of sides.

CHICKEN CORDON BLEU

While very French, Chicken Cordon Bleu influenced American dining and became a classic, being served across the nation! I wanted to pay tribute to this famous entree and give it a try in the air fryer. The results are just as good as the original and it's quite straightforward! Just a little prep work, then let your air fryer do the rest. Served with a simple bechamel sauce and your favorite vegetable, this is a great date night meal!

COOK TIME: 16 MIN | EFFORT: MODERATE

INGREDIENTS

- 2 boneless skinless chicken breasts
- 1 tablespoon (15 g) Dijon mustard
- 1 tablespoon (15 ml) honey
- ½ teaspoon salt
- ¼ teaspoon pepper
- 4 slices Swiss cheese
- 4 slices ham
- ¼ cup (32 g) flour
- 1 egg
- 1 cup (68 g) panko breadcrumbs
- ⅓ cup (32 g) grated Parmesan cheese
  Oil spray

SAUCE

- 2 tablespoons (28 g) butter
- 2 tablespoons (16 g) flour
- 1 cup (236 ml) milk
- ¼ teaspoon salt
- ¼ teaspoon pepper
  Pinch nutmeg

DIRECTIONS

1. Cut the chicken in half lengthwise, leaving the breast attached at one side. Open the breast, cover with plastic wrap, and using a meat mallet, pound the chicken to ¼-inch thick. Repeat with the remaining breast.

2. In a small bowl, combine the mustard and honey. Season the chicken breasts with salt and pepper then spread the honey mustard sauce in the middle. Lay one slice of cheese in each breast, then top with two slices of ham and one more slice of cheese. Roll each breast closed and secure with a toothpick.

3. Preheat the air fryer to 350° F (170° C). In a shallow bowl, add the flour, in another shallow bowl, beat the egg, and in another shallow bowl, mix together the panko and Parmesan.

4. Dip the chicken in the flour, then egg, and finally, roll in the panko mixture. Spray the air fryer with oil, add the chicken, spray with oil, and cook for 12-16 minutes, flipping halfway through and spraying with more oil.

5. Meanwhile, in a small saucepan over medium heat, melt the butter. Whisk in the flour, stirring continuously for 2 minutes. Gradually, add in the milk, stirring after each addition. Add in the salt, pepper, and nutmeg, stirring until combined.

6. Slice the chicken and serve topped with sauce and your choice of side.

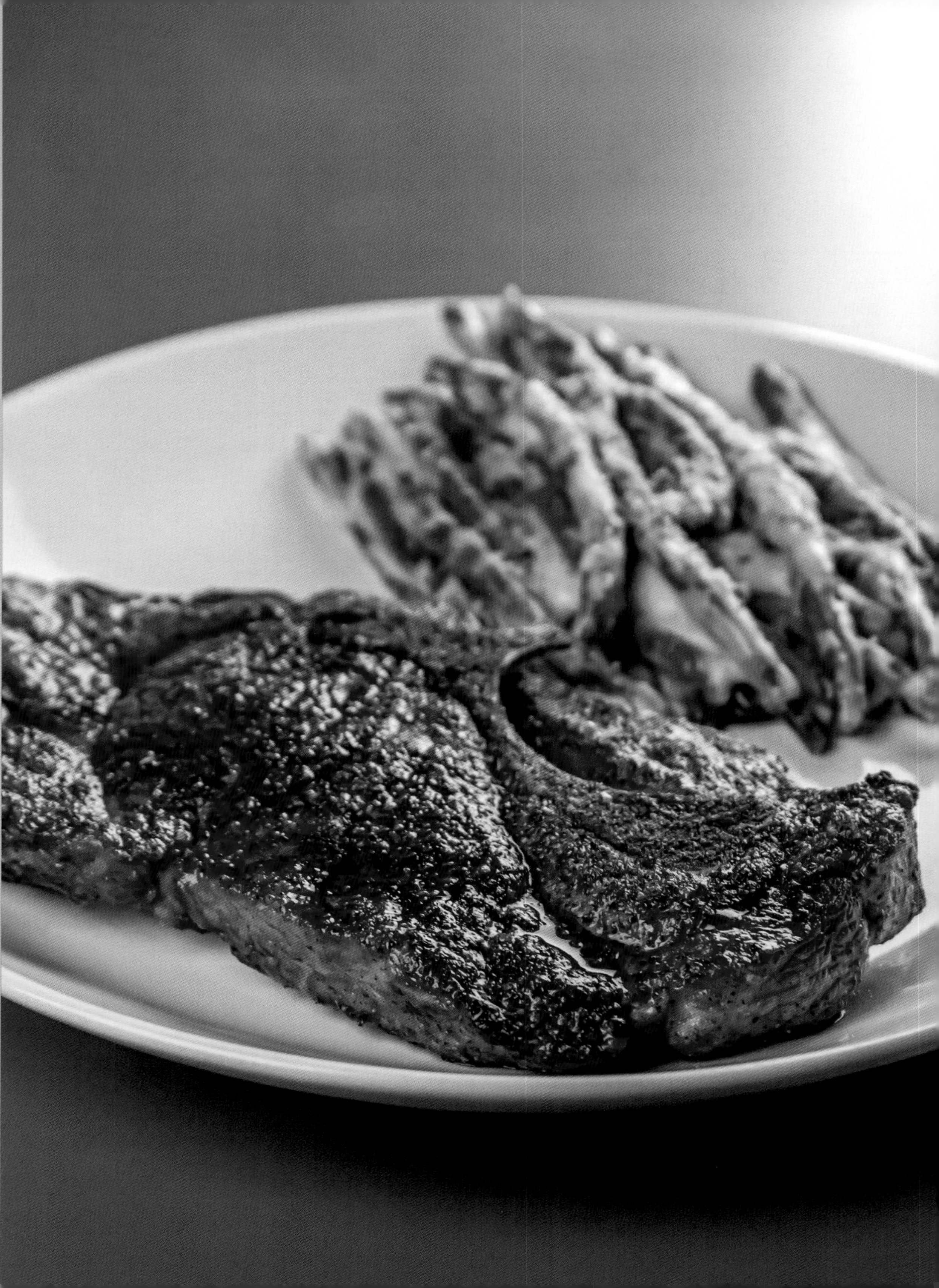

ROASTED PORK STEAKS AND CREAMED GREEN BEANS

While perhaps not as popular as the pork chop, pork steaks are well-deserving of some of the limelight. Made from shoulder roast that is sliced into steaks, they're often more forgiving and more flavorful than the chop. They cook perfectly in the air fryer and a sprinkling of seasoning is all you need to have a dinner fit for a king (or queen!)

COOK TIME: 26 MIN | EFFORT: EASY

BEANS

- 1 pound (452 g) green beans, trimmed
- ½ teaspoon salt
- ¼ teaspoon pepper
- 1 tablespoon (14 g) butter
- 2 teaspoons (5 g) flour
- ¼ teaspoons onion powder
- ¼ teaspoons garlic powder
  Salt and pepper, to taste
- ½ cup (118 g) milk
- 2 tablespoons (12 g) grated Parmesan cheese

INGREDIENTS

- 2 (8-ounce [227 g]) bone-in pork steaks
- 1 teaspoon salt
- ½ teaspoon pepper
- 1 teaspoon onion powder
- 1 teaspoon garlic powder
- 1 teaspoon chili powder
  Oil spray

DIRECTIONS

1. Preheat the air fryer to 400° F (200° C). Place the green beans in the air fryer, spray with oil, season with salt and pepper, and stir to coat. Cook for 8-12 minutes, stirring halfway through. Set aside.

2. To prepare the steaks: In a small bowl, combine the salt, pepper, onion powder, and garlic powder. Sprinkle over the pork steaks on both sides. Spray the air fryer with oil, add a pork steak, spray with oil, cook one at a time for 10-14 minutes, flipping halfway through.

3. Meanwhile, in a small saucepan over medium heat, melt the butter. Whisk in the flour, stirring continuously for 2 minutes. Gradually, add in the milk, stirring after each addition. Add in the salt, pepper, onion powder, and garlic powder, stirring until combined. Continue stirring until the mixture begins to thicken, then add the Parmesan. Add the green beans and continue stirring until the beans are warmed through. Serve alongside the pork.

ROAST BEEF WITH HERBED CARROTS AND POTATOES

When it comes to comfort food, for me, not much can top a roast beef. Normally made with a large chunk of meat, roast beef is often fit for a larger crowd or gathering, but the air fryer changes all of that! You can have this comfort food staple and have just enough for two!

COOK TIME: 1 HR 30 MIN | EFFORT: EASY

INGREDIENTS

- 1 teaspoon garlic powder
- 1 teaspoon onion powder
- 1 teaspoon dried parsley
- 1 teaspoon dried thyme
- 1 teaspoon dried basil
- ½ teaspoon salt
- ¼ teaspoon pepper
- 1 (8-ounce [227 g]) beef roast
- 1 tablespoon (15 ml) canola oil
- 8 ounces (227 g) red skin potatoes, quartered
- 2 large carrots, sliced

DIRECTIONS

1. Preheat the air fryer to 390° F (190° C). In a small bowl, combine the garlic powder, onion powder, parsley, thyme, basil, salt, and pepper. Rub the roast with the oil then rub half of the herb mixture over the entire roast.

2. Place the roast in the air fryer and cook for 12-16 minutes. Flip the roast over and reduce the temperature to 360° F (180° C). Cook for another 50-60 minutes, or until a thermometer reads desired doneness.

3. Meanwhile, in a large bowl, add the potatoes, carrots, and remaining herb mix, spray with oil, tossing to coat. After 45 minutes of cooking, add the carrots and potatoes, and continue cooking for the remaining 15 minutes.

4. Allow the roast to rest, covered with foil, for 15 minutes before slicing and serving with the potatoes and carrots.

(UN)TRADITIONAL FRIED CHICKEN

Does anything hit the spot like fried chicken? The air fryer removes the guilt from this guilty pleasure while sacrificing nothing! To get the crispy exterior you're used to, you will still need some oil but it's substantially less than if you were deep-frying it.

COOK TIME: 14 MIN | EFFORT: EASY

INGREDIENTS

- 1 teaspoon salt
- 1 teaspoon pepper
- 1 teaspoon garlic powder
- 1 teaspoon paprika
- ½ teaspoon onion powder
- ½ teaspoon Italian seasoning
- 4 chicken leg drumsticks
- ½ cup (68 g) flour
- ½ teaspoon baking powder
- 2 tablespoons (15 g) cornstarch
- 1 egg
- 2 teaspoons (10 ml) hot sauce
- 3 tablespoons (44 ml) milk
- Oil spray

DIRECTIONS

1. In a small bowl, combine the salt, pepper, garlic powder, paprika, onion powder, and Italian seasoning. Season the chicken with half of the spice mixture and set aside.

2. In a large resealable bag, mix together the flour, baking powder, cornstarch, and the remaining spice mix. In a medium bowl, beat the egg, hot sauce, and milk together.

3. Place the chicken in the flour mixture and shake to coat. Dip the chicken into the egg mixture, then return to the flour mixture. Transfer the chicken to a plate and allow the chicken to rest for 15 minutes.

4. Preheat the air fryer to 350° F (170° C). Spray the air fryer with oil, add the chicken, and spray thoroughly with oil. Cook for 10-14 minutes, flipping halfway through and spraying with additional oil. Rest for 5 minutes before serving.

GARLIC AND HERB PORK TENDERLOIN

Juicy, herb-crusted tenderloin is sliced and served with seasoned potatoes. What gets better than that? I'm glad you asked! It all comes together at the same time in your air fryer. Making the most of your time, while still delivering a flavorful meal!

COOK TIME: 22 MIN | EFFORT: EASY

INGREDIENTS

- ½ teaspoon salt
- ½ teaspoon onion powder
- ¼ teaspoon pepper
- ¼ teaspoon paprika
- ¼ teaspoon chili powder
- 2 garlic cloves, minced
- 1 teaspoon dried parsley
- ½ teaspoon (2 ml) canola oil
- 1 (8-ounce [227 g]) pork tenderloin

POTATOES

- 1 pound (452 g) small potatoes, quartered
- 1 teaspoon (5 ml) canola oil
- ½ teaspoon dried parsley
- 2 garlic cloves, minced
- ½ teaspoon salt
- ¼ teaspoon pepper

DIRECTIONS

1. Preheat the air fryer to 400° F (200° C). In a small bowl, combine the salt, onion powder, pepper, paprika, chili powder, garlic, and parsley. Rub the tenderloin with the oil then rub with the herb mixture over the entire tenderloin.

2. In a medium bowl, add the potatoes, oil, parsley, garlic, salt, and pepper, tossing to coat.

3. Spray the air fryer with oil, add the tenderloin and potatoes, and cook for 18-22 minutes, flipping halfway through. Allow the pork to rest, wrapped in foil, for 15 minutes before slicing and serving.

KIELBASA AND VEGETABLE STIR FRY

While the idea of kielbasa, peppers, and onions being served on a bed of rice may sound a bit strange, this dish absolutely works. It's one of my "in a pinch" meals because it takes little effort to come together but has a big flavor! But don't just take my word for it, give it a try!

COOK TIME: 18 MIN | EFFORT: EASY

INGREDIENTS

- 1 cup (195 g) uncooked rice
- 1 small onion, thinly sliced
- 1 small green pepper, thinly sliced
- 1 (12-ounce [340 g]) package kielbasa, sliced
- 1 tablespoon (15 ml) Worcestershire sauce
- 1 tablespoon (15 ml) low-sodium soy sauce
- ½ cup (118 ml) water
  Oil spray

DIRECTIONS

1. Preheat the air fryer to 400° F (200° C).

2. In a small saucepan, cook rice according to the package directions.

3. Meanwhile, spray the air fryer with oil and add the onions and peppers. Lay the kielbasa over the top, spray with oil, and cook for 10-14 minutes, stirring halfway through.

4. In a large pan over medium-high heat, add the sausage mixture, Worcestershire sauce, soy sauce, and water, cooking for 3-4 minutes, or until slightly reduced. Serve over rice.

SANTA FE STEAK SALAD

Does it get any more American than throwing a steak on salad and calling it a meal? Whoever came up with the idea is a genius in my opinion, though. While I have had many steak salads, this one is one of my favorites! Inspired by the bold flavors of Santa Fe, this salad has all the makings for a delicious and satisfying meal.

COOK TIME: 10 MIN | EFFORT: EASY

DRESSING

- ¼ cup (59 ml) prepared ranch
- 2 tablespoons (29 g) salsa
- ¼ teaspoon hot sauce
- ¼ teaspoon paprika
- ⅛ teaspoon cayenne pepper
- ¼ teaspoon ground cumin

INGREDIENTS

- ¼ teaspoon pepper
- 2 teaspoons (3 g) taco seasoning
- 1 (8-ounce [227 g]) skirt steak
- 1 (6-ounce [170 g]) bag baby spinach
- 1 (10-ounce [283.5 g]) bag lettuce
- 1 (15-ounce [425 g]) can black beans, rinsed and drained
- 1 (8-ounce [227 g]) can sliced black olives
- 1 avocado peeled, pitted, and sliced
- 1 cup (136 g) grape tomatoes, halved
- 1 (15-ounce [425 g]) can hominy, drained
- 1 cup (112 g) shredded cheddar cheese
- ¼ cup (11 g) chopped fresh cilantro
- 1 lime, cut into wedges

DIRECTIONS

1. In a medium bowl, stir together the ranch, salsa, hot sauce, paprika, cayenne, and cumin. Cover and refrigerate.

2. Preheat the air fryer to 400° F (200° C).

3. In a small bowl, combine the pepper and taco seasoning. Season the steak on both sides. Spray the air fryer with oil, add the steak, spray with oil, and cook for 6-10 minutes, flipping halfway through. Let rest for 10 minutes before slicing into strips, cutting across the grain.

4. Meanwhile, assemble the salad with spinach, lettuce, black beans, olives, avocado, tomatoes, hominy, and cheese. Top with the sliced steak, cilantro, and a lime wedge. Serve with the dressing on the side.

CRISPY CHICKEN TENDER SALAD WITH RANCH

A simple salad can be transformed into one satisfying meal when you top with these delicious chicken tenders! Okay, you're right, a salad can totally be a meal without the chicken tenders but these are so good, you'll want them anyway! Served with homemade ranch, this will challenge even the best salad at your favorite restaurant!

COOK TIME: 14 MIN | EFFORT: EASY

DRESSING

- 2 tablespoons (30 ml) mayo
- 2 tablespoons (30 ml) sour cream
- 2 tablespoons (30 ml) milk
- ¼ teaspoons garlic powder
- ¼ teaspoons onion powder
- ¼ teaspoons dried parsley
- Salt and pepper, to taste

INGREDIENTS

- 1 teaspoon salt
- 1 teaspoon pepper
- 1 teaspoon garlic powder
- 1 teaspoon paprika
- ½ teaspoon onion powder
- ½ teaspoon Italian seasoning
- 2 chicken breasts, sliced into strips
- ½ cup (68 g) flour
- ½ teaspoon baking powder
- 2 tablespoons (15 g) cornstarch
- 1 egg
- 3 tablespoons (45 ml) milk
- Oil spray
- 1 cup shredded cheese, of choice
- 1 bag prepared tossed salad kit
- ½ cup (28 g) crispy fried onions

DIRECTIONS

1. In a small bowl, combine the mayo, sour cream, milk, garlic powder, onion powder, parsley, salt, and pepper. Cover and refrigerate.

2. In another small bowl, combine the salt, pepper, garlic powder, paprika, onion powder, and Italian seasoning. Season the chicken with half of the spice mixture and set aside.

3. In a large resealable bag, mix together the flour, baking powder, cornstarch, and the remaining spice mix. In a shallow bowl, beat the egg and milk together.

4. Place the chicken in the flour mixture and shake until fully coated. Dip the chicken into the egg mixture, then return to the flour mixture. Transfer the chicken to a plate and allow the chicken to rest for 15 minutes.

5. Preheat the air fryer to 350° F (170° C). Spray the air fryer with oil, add the chicken, and spray thoroughly with oil. Cook for 10-14 minutes, flipping halfway through and spraying with more oil. Once done, let rest for 5 minutes before slicing.

6. Meanwhile, assemble each bowl with half of the salad mix, cheese, onions, and chicken. Serve with the ranch.

THE CATCH
OF THE DAY

The air fryer is known for making healthier upgrades to your favorite fried foods, but if I'm honest, I had some skepticism when it came to my favorite fried fishes. But, if this chapter's presence doesn't give it away, I was pleasantly surprised with just how great all of these came out! Of course, I included your favorite breaded fish, but you can also roast salmon or even make fish tacos!

SEASONED FISH TACOS WITH SPICY MANGO SALSA

If you're not sure how you feel about fish or just prefer a milder flavor, these fish tacos are perfect for you! Made with orange roughy, a mild-flavored fish, and served with a sweet mango salsa; these tacos will make for an anything-but-boring dinner.

COOK TIME: 12 MIN | EFFORT: EASY

SALSA

- ⅓ cup (83 g) mango preserves
- 1 small tomato, diced
- 1 small jalapeño, diced
- 1 small red pepper, diced
- 1 tablespoon (3 g) cilantro, chopped
- 1 small red onion, diced
- 2 teaspoons (8 g) sugar
- 1 teaspoon salt
- ½ teaspoon garlic powder

INGREDIENTS

- ½ teaspoon paprika
- ½ teaspoon chili powder
- ½ teaspoon salt
- ¼ teaspoon pepper
- 2 (6-ounce [170 g]) orange roughy fillets, or other mild white fish
- Shaved cabbage, for serving
- Sour cream, for serving
- 6 (6-inch) tortillas

DIRECTIONS

1. In a small bowl, stir together the mango, tomatoes, jalapeños, peppers, cilantro, red onions, sugar, salt, and garlic powder; cover and refrigerate.

2. Preheat the air fryer to 380° F (190° C).

3. In a small bowl, combine the paprika, chili powder, salt, and pepper. Season the fish on both sides with the spice mixture. Spray the air fryer with oil, add the fish, spray with oil, and cook for 8-12 minutes, flipping halfway through.

4. Using a fork, flake the fish into large pieces. Fill the tortillas with the fish, cabbage, and sour cream, topping with the mango salsa.

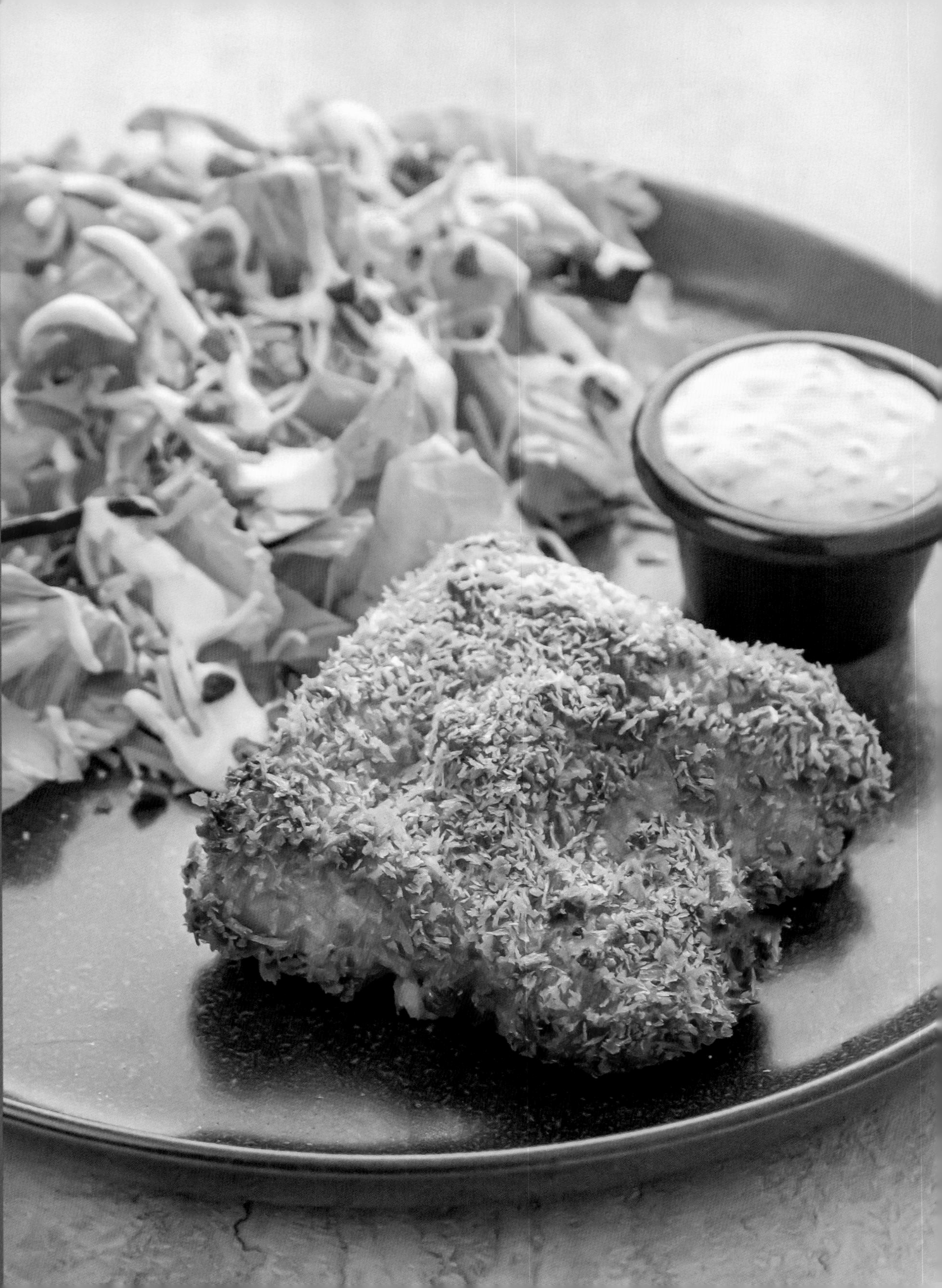

CRISPY FISH FILLETS WITH TARTAR SAUCE

If you know anything about the air fryer, you know that making healthy versions of fried foods is its claim to fame. This is definitely the case here with these crispy fish fillets coated in crunchy panko breadcrumbs. Serve them with the potato wedges on page 159 for a healthy twist on fish and chips!

COOK TIME: 12 MIN | EFFORT: EASY

SAUCE

- ¼ cup (55 g) mayo
- 1 tablespoon (15 g) sweet relish
- ⅛ teaspoon onion powder
- ⅛ teaspoon dried dill weed
- ½ teaspoon lemon juice
- Salt, to taste

INGREDIENTS

- ¼ cup (33 g) flour
- 1 teaspoon paprika
- ¼ teaspoon garlic powder
- ¼ teaspoon salt
- ⅛ teaspoon pepper
- 1 egg
- ½ cup (54 g) panko breadcrumbs
- 2 (6-ounce [170 g]) cod fillets
- Lemon wedges, optional, for serving
- Oil spray

DIRECTIONS

1. In a small bowl, stir together the mayo, relish, onion powder, dill, lemon juice, and salt until fully combined; set aside.

2. Preheat the air fryer to 400° F (200° C).

3. In a small bowl, stir together the flour, paprika, garlic powder, salt, and pepper. In a shallow bowl, beat the egg. In another shallow bowl, add the panko.

4. Pat the fish dry, coat each fillet in the flour mixture, then the egg, and the panko, pressing down lightly to ensure they stick. Spray the air fryer with oil, add the fish, spray with oil, and cook for 8-12 minutes, until crispy and a light golden color. Serve with the prepared tartar sauce and enjoy!

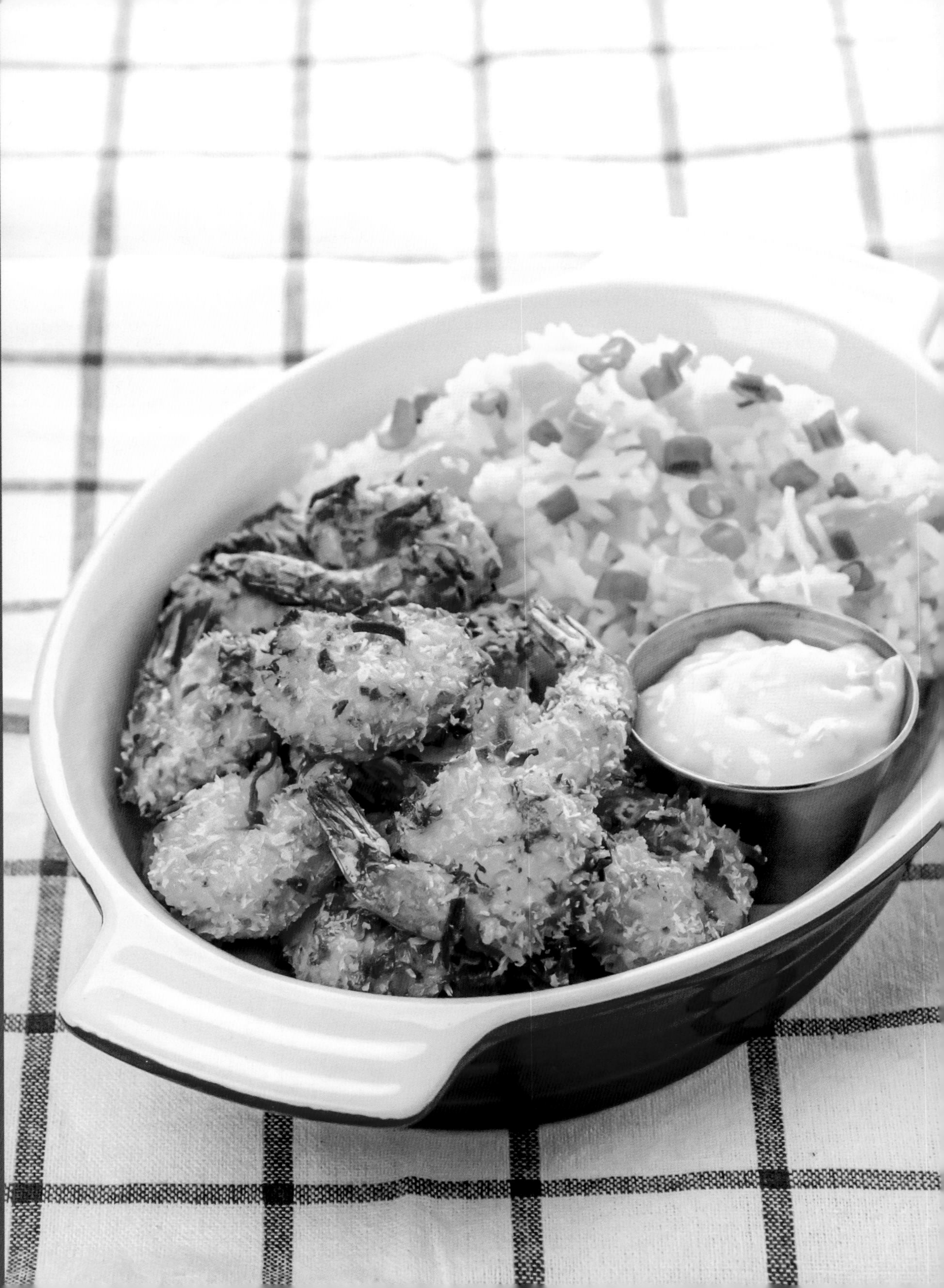

COCONUT SHRIMP WITH TROPICAL RICE

I love the subtle sweetness of coconut shrimp and wondered if it could be made in an air fryer and taste just as good. It turns out, it absolutely can! To turn this into a complete meal, though, I paired it with tropical-flavored rice made with shredded coconut (of course!) and pineapple preserves which do double duty in the dipping sauce as well!

COOK TIME: 12 MIN | EFFORT: EASY

SAUCE

- 1 (6-ounce [170 g]) container vanilla yogurt
- 1 tablespoon (20 g) pineapple preserves
- 1 tablespoon (6 g) shredded sweetened coconut

RICE

- 1 cup (195 g) uncooked rice
- 3 tablespoons (60 g) pineapple preserves
- 2 tablespoons (12 g) shredded sweetened coconut
- 2 green onions, sliced, dark green parts reserved for garnish

INGREDIENTS

- 2 tablespoons (16 g) flour
- ½ teaspoon salt
- ¼ teaspoon pepper
- ¼ cup (27 g) panko breadcrumbs
- ¼ cup (24 g) shredded sweetened coconut
- 1 egg
- 8 ounces (227 g) shrimp, peeled, deveined, and tails removed

DIRECTIONS

1. In a small bowl, stir together the yogurt, pineapple preserves, and coconut. Refrigerate until serving.

2. In a medium saucepan, cook the rice according to the package directions, adding the pineapple, coconut, and onion with the rice.

3. Meanwhile, in a resealable bag, combine the flour, salt, and pepper. In a small bowl, combine the panko and coconut. In a shallow bowl, beat the egg.

4. Preheat the air fryer to 400° F (200° C). Add the shrimp to the flour mixture and shake to coat. Dip each shrimp in the egg, then into the coconut mixture. Add the shrimp to the air fryer, spray with oil, and cook for 8-12 minutes, flipping halfway through.

5. Serve the shrimp alongside the pineapple rice and the sauce for dipping.

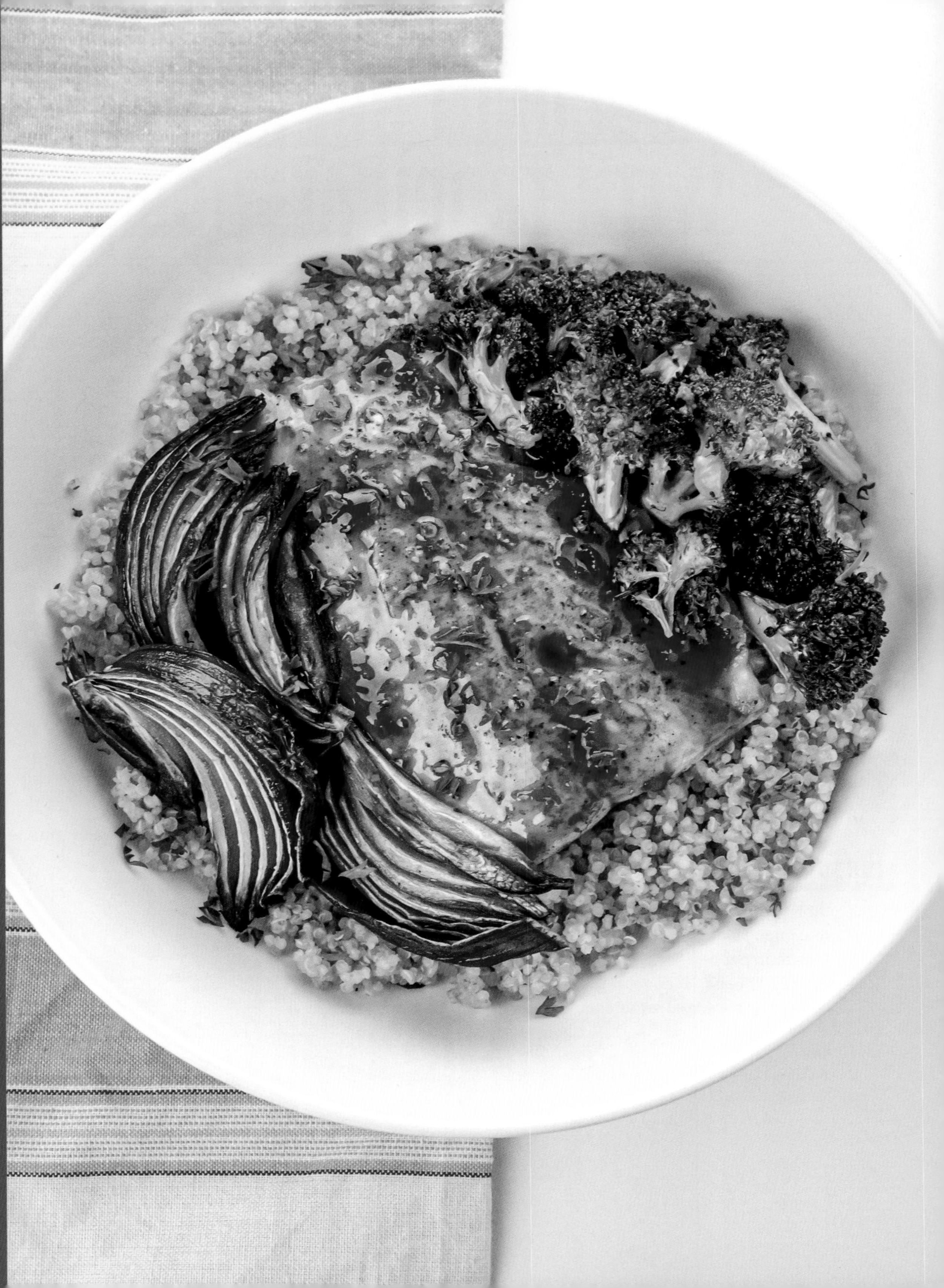

SALMON WITH QUINOA AND WEDGED ONION

This beautiful dish comes together so easily, you just might feel guilty! Who am I kidding, there's zero guilt here. Salmon gets coated in an Asian-inspired, two-ingredient glaze, and tops a bowl full of protein-packed quinoa and roasted vegetables making for one truly satisfying dinner.

COOK TIME: 18 MIN | EFFORT: EASY

INGREDIENTS

- 1 small head broccoli, cut into florets
- 1 small red onion, quartered
- ½ cup (85 g) quinoa
- 2 (6-ounce) salmon fillets
- ½ teaspoon salt
- ¼ teaspoon pepper
- ¼ teaspoon paprika
- 2 tablespoons (35 g) sweet chili sauce
- 1½ tablespoons (23 ml) low-sodium soy sauce
- Oil spray

DIRECTIONS

1. Preheat the air fryer to 400° F (200° C). Add the broccoli and onions to the air fryer, spray with oil, and cook for 4-6 minutes.

2. In a medium saucepan, cook the quinoa according to the package directions.

3. Meanwhile, season the salmon with salt, pepper, and paprika. Stir the broccoli and onions, spray with additional oil, and place the salmon on top, cooking for 8-12 minutes.

4. In a small bowl, stir together the chili sauce and soy sauce, and carefully spread it over the salmon.

5. Layer the quinoa and vegetables in two serving bowls, and top with the salmon and any remaining sauce.

ROASTED SALMON SALAD WITH ASIAN DRESSING

I always prepare salmon with Asian flavors; I can't place why but it's just my favorite way to prepare it. Sticking with this tradition comes this salad. Besides the edamame, the fixings aren't really out of the ordinary for a salad, but the Asian dressing is what gives this salad its Asian flavor inspiration.

COOK TIME: 10 MIN | EFFORT: EASY

DRESSING

- 2 tablespoons (30 ml) low-sodium soy sauce
- 1½ teaspoons (8 ml) toasted sesame oil
- 1 tablespoon (15 ml) white vinegar
- 1 tablespoon (15 ml) sweet chili sauce
- 2 tablespoons (30 ml) canola oil
- 2 teaspoons (10 ml) honey
- ¼ teaspoon powdered ginger
- ¼ teaspoon garlic powder

INGREDIENTS

- 2 (6-ounce [170 g]) salmon fillets
- ½ teaspoon salt
- ¼ teaspoon pepper
- 1 (9-ounce [255 g]) bag romaine lettuce
- 1 handful baby spinach, optional
- 1 small cucumber, halved and sliced
- ½ cup (73 g) cherry tomatoes, halved
- 1 avocado, diced
- ½ cup (78 g) frozen edamame
- 1 small red onion, thinly sliced
- ¼ cup (11 g) chopped cilantro

DIRECTIONS

1. Preheat the air fryer to 390° F (190° C).

2. In a small bowl, stir together the soy sauce, sesame oil, vinegar, sweet chili sauce, oil, honey, ginger, and garlic powder; set aside.

3. Season the salmon with salt and pepper, place in the air fryer, spray with oil, and cook for 6-10 minutes.

4. Meanwhile, in two serving bowls, layer the romaine, spinach, cucumber, tomatoes, avocado, edamame, and red onion. Top each salad with one salmon fillet and a sprinkle of cilantro. Serve with dressing on the side.

CRISPY SHRIMP SALAD WITH ZESTY DRESSING

This salad is inspired by the Shrimp Louie, a traditional salad from California, but with some creative liberties. Crispy, air-fried shrimp add great textural contrast! I also excluded the hardboiled eggs, but you certainly can add them. Served with a dressing similar to thousand island, this is one satisfying salad!

COOK TIME: 22 MIN | EFFORT: EASY

DRESSING

- 2 tablespoons (27 g) mayo
- 2 tablespoons (30 ml) chili sauce, or ketchup
- 2 dashes hot sauce
- 1 teaspoon lemon juice
- ½ teaspoon apple cider vinegar
- ½ teaspoon brown sugar
- ½ teaspoon paprika
- Salt, to taste

INGREDIENTS

- 3 ounces (85 g) fresh green beans, trimmed and cut into thirds
- Salt, to taste
- ½ teaspoon Chesapeake bay seasoning, such as Old Bay®
- ½ teaspoon seasoning salt
- ¼ teaspoon onion powder
- ¼ teaspoon garlic powder
- 1 egg
- ½ cup (54 g) panko bread crumbs
- 8 ounces (227 g) shrimp, peeled, deveined, and tails removed
- 1 (10-ounce [284 g]) bag romaine lettuce
- ½ English cucumber, sliced
- ½ cup (73 g) cherry tomatoes
- 3 radishes, sliced
- ½ cup (77 g) black olives, whole
- Oil spray

DIRECTIONS

1. In a small bowl, stir together the mayo, chili sauce, hot sauce, lemon juice, vinegar, brown sugar, paprika, and salt; cover and refrigerate.

2. Preheat the air fryer to 400° F (200° C). Add the green beans, spray with oil, season with salt, and cook for 10 minutes, stirring halfway through; set aside to cool.

3. Meanwhile, in a small bowl, combine the Chesapeake Bay, seasoning salt, onion powder, and garlic powder. In a shallow bowl, beat the egg. In another shallow bowl, add the panko.

4. Season the shrimp with the seasoning mixture, dip into the egg, and then panko. Spray the air fryer with oil, add the shrimp, spray with oil, and cook for 8-12 minutes, flipping halfway through and spraying with more oil.

5. In two serving bowls, layer the romaine, cucumber, tomatoes, radishes, and olives. Top each salad with shrimp and serve with the dressing on the side.

CRAB CAKES WITH TARTAR SAUCE

Crab cakes may not be the first thing you think of for a main entree but let's be different! Perfectly seasoned and loaded with protein, these cakes can be quite versatile! Serve them with a delicious salad or along with a linguine alfredo for a satisfying dinner.

COOK TIME: 12 MIN | EFFORT: EASY

SAUCE

- ¼ cup (55 g) mayo
- 1 tablespoon (15 g) sweet relish
- ⅛ teaspoon onion powder
- ⅛ teaspoon dried dill weed
- ½ teaspoon lemon juice
- Salt, to taste

INGREDIENTS

- 2 (6-ounce [170 g]) cans lump crab, drained
- 2 tablespoons (27 g) mayo
- 1 egg yolk
- 2 teaspoons (11 g) Dijon mustard
- 1 green onion, diced
- ¼ teaspoon salt
- ⅛ teaspoon pepper
- ¼ teaspoon seasoning salt
- ¼ teaspoon onion powder
- ½ teaspoon Chesapeake bay seasoning, such as Old Bay®
- ¼ cup (27 g) panko breadcrumbs
- Oil spray

DIRECTIONS

1. In a small bowl, stir together the mayo, relish, onion powder, dill, lemon juice, and salt until fully combined.

2. Preheat the air fryer to 350° F (170° C).

3. In a large bowl, stir together the crab, mayo, egg yolk, mustard, green onion, salt, pepper, seasoning salt, onion powder, and Chesapeake bay seasoning. Divide the mixture into four equal balls and form them into patties. Thoroughly coat the patties in the panko.

4. Spray the air fryer with oil, add the crab cakes, spray with oil, and cook for 8-12 minutes, flipping halfway through. Serve with the prepared tartar sauce and enjoy!

SHAREABLES

AND SIDES

Cooking for two is not always easy; it can be challenging finding recipes that don't feed a crowd. I'm not sure this pain is worse than when it comes to appetizers and sides. So I've taken some of my favorite appetizers and sides, compiled them into this great chapter dedicated to some of our favorite finger foods. Enjoy everything from dips to eggrolls and, everyone's favorite restaurant appetizer, onion blossom petals!

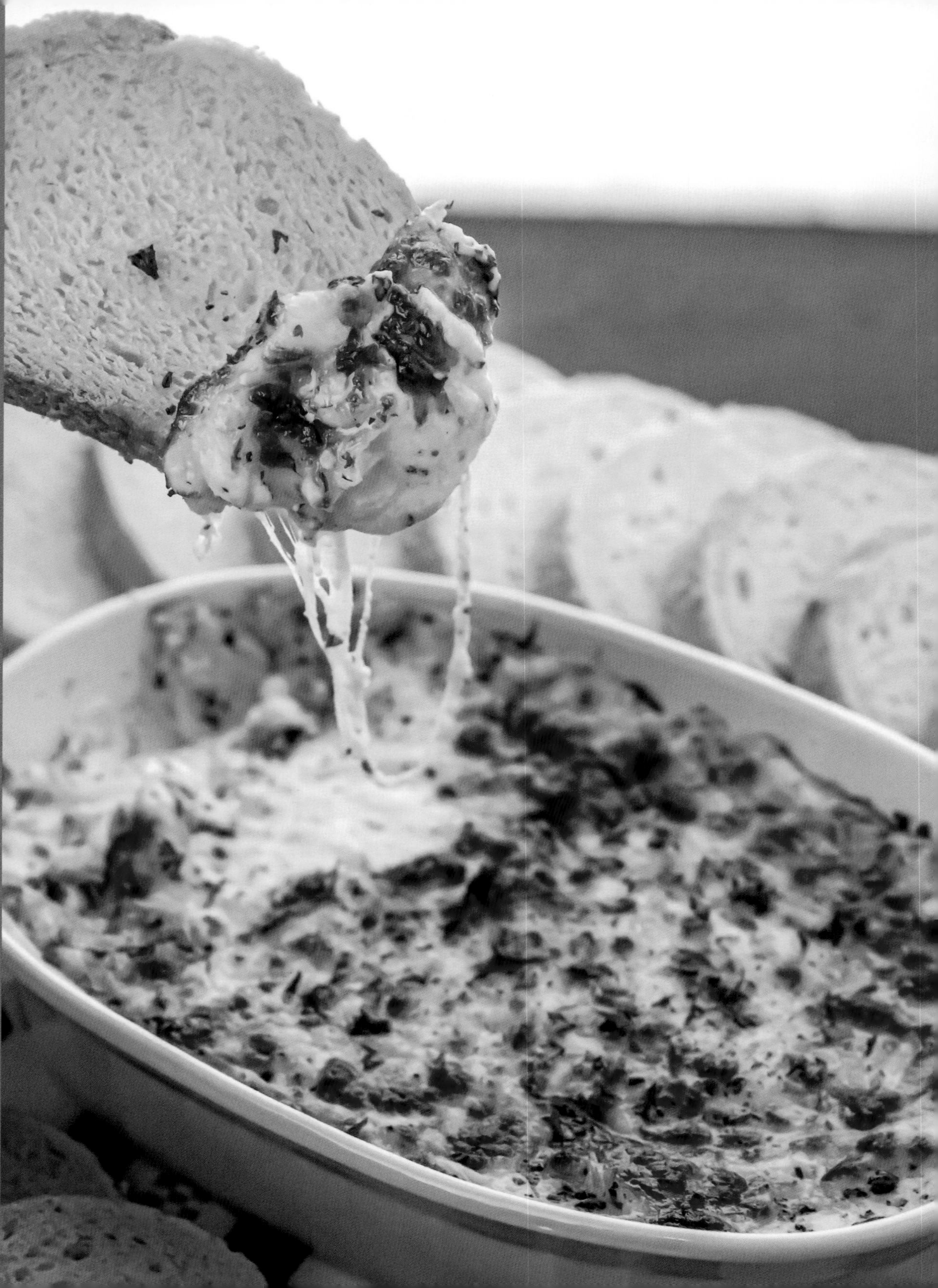

CHEESY BAKED RICOTTA DIP

If you're looking for a simple yet show-stopping appetizer, look no further than this baked ricotta dip! Simply combine the ingredients and bake it in the air fryer. It's an Italian-inspired appetizer even your Nonna will approve of!

COOK TIME: 17 MIN | EFFORT: EASY

INGREDIENTS

- 1 cup (246 g) ricotta
- ½ teaspoon garlic powder
- ½ teaspoon onion powder
- 1 teaspoon Italian seasoning
- ½ teaspoon salt
- ¼ teaspoon pepper
- ¼ cup (28 g) mozzarella
- ¼ cup (24 g) grated Parmesan cheese
- Dried parsley, for garnish
- ½ French baguette, sliced
- Oil spray

DIRECTIONS

1. Preheat the air fryer to 400° F (200° C).

2. In a medium bowl, stir together the ricotta, garlic powder, onion powder, Italian seasoning, salt, pepper, mozzarella, and Parmesan. Spray a 6-inch baking dish with oil, add the cheese mixture, and sprinkle with parsley. Cover with foil, place in the air fryer, and bake for 8-12 minutes.

3. Carefully remove the foil and cook for 3-5 minutes more until the cheese has browned. Serve with baguette slices.

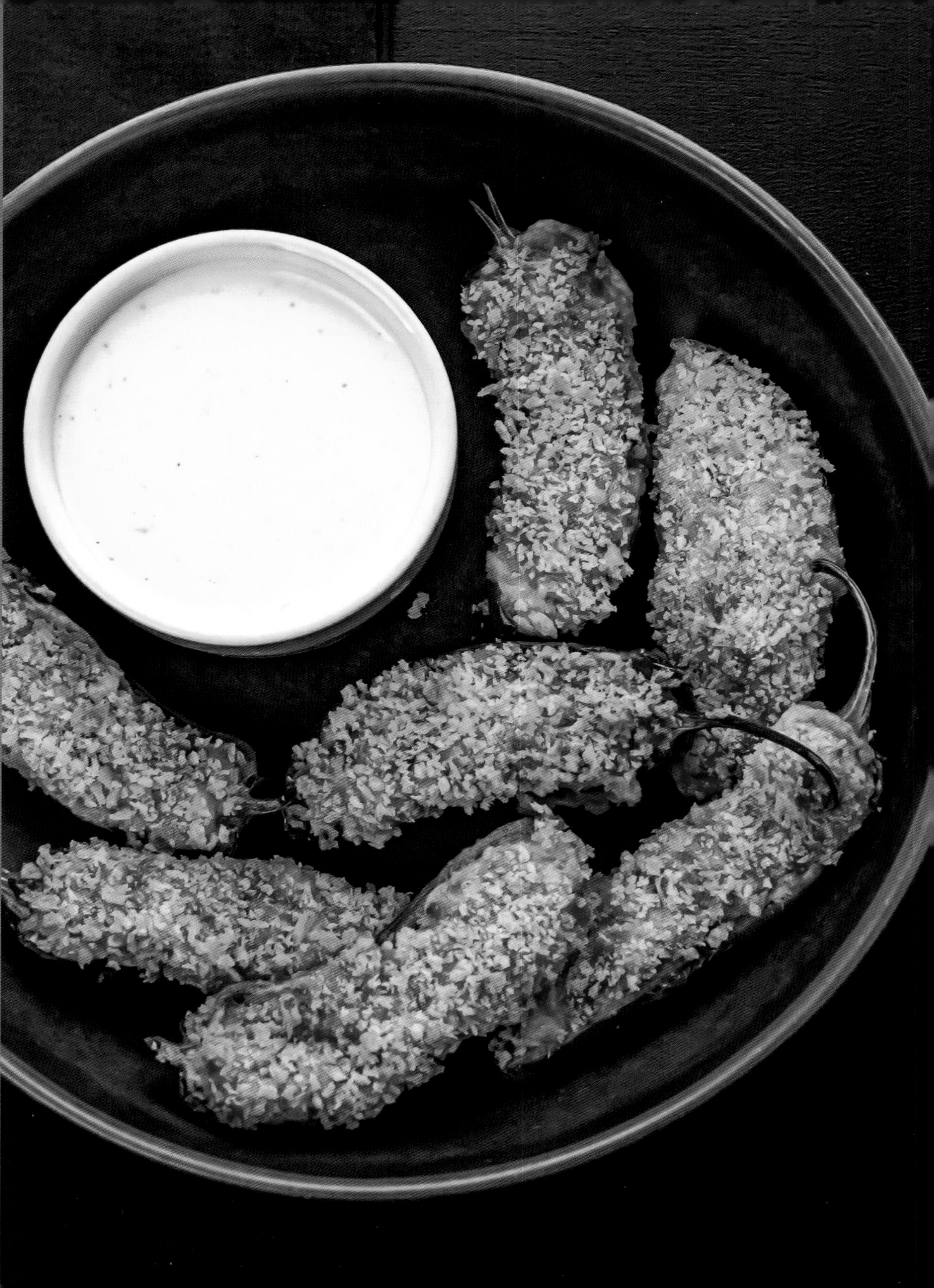

PANKO-DIPPED JALAPEÑO POPPERS

There's something about the finger food appetizers that are just downright fun to eat! Jalapeño poppers are no exception, and I don't think they get any easier to make than this. Just cut them, fill them, and dip them! You're on your way to fun and flavorful appetizer!

COOK TIME: 10 MIN | EFFORT: EASY

INGREDIENTS

- ½ cup (116 g) cream cheese, softened
- ½ cup (56 g) shredded cheddar cheese
- 1 teaspoon paprika
- 2 tablespoons (25 g) bacon bits
- ½ cup (54 g) panko breadcrumbs
- 6 large jalapeño peppers, halved lengthwise, seeds and membranes removed
- Oil spray

DIRECTIONS

1. Preheat the air fryer to 400° F (200° C).

2. In a medium bowl, stir together the cream cheese, cheddar, paprika, and bacon until fully combined. In a shallow bowl, add the breadcrumbs. Fill each jalapeño half with the cheese mixture, then dip into the panko. Place them in the air fryer, spray with oil, and cook for 6-10 minutes.

3. Serve as an appetizer dipped in your favorite sauce before dinner.

CRAB RANGOON EGGROLLS WITH SWEET SOY SAUCE

If you love crab rangoons, you're going to love how easy these are to make. Now, I love them crispy, but the edges get a little too crunchy when folding them the traditional way. The solution? Make them into eggrolls!

COOK TIME: 10 MIN | EFFORT: EASY

INGREDIENTS

- ½ cup (116 g) cream cheese, softened
- 1 green onion, sliced
- 1 teaspoon Worcestershire sauce
- 1 (6-ounce [170 g]) can crab meat, drained
- 6 eggroll wrappers
- 1 tablespoon (15 ml) sweet chili sauce
- 2 teaspoons (10 ml) low-sodium soy sauce

DIRECTIONS

1. In a small bowl, stir together the cream cheese, green onion, Worcestershire, and crab.

2. On a work surface, lay an eggroll wrapper in a diamond shape. Scoop 2 tablespoon of the crab mixture into the middle of the wrapper. Fold in the bottom, left, and right corners, gently pressing to remove any air bubbles. Using your finger, brush the top corner with water, and roll up to seal. Place it seam side down and repeat with the remaining eggrolls.

3. Preheat the air fryer to 320° F (160° C). Spray the air fryer with oil, add the eggrolls, spray with oil, and cook for 6-10 minutes, flipping halfway through.

4. Meanwhile, in a small bowl, combine the chili sauce and soy sauce. Serve with eggrolls.

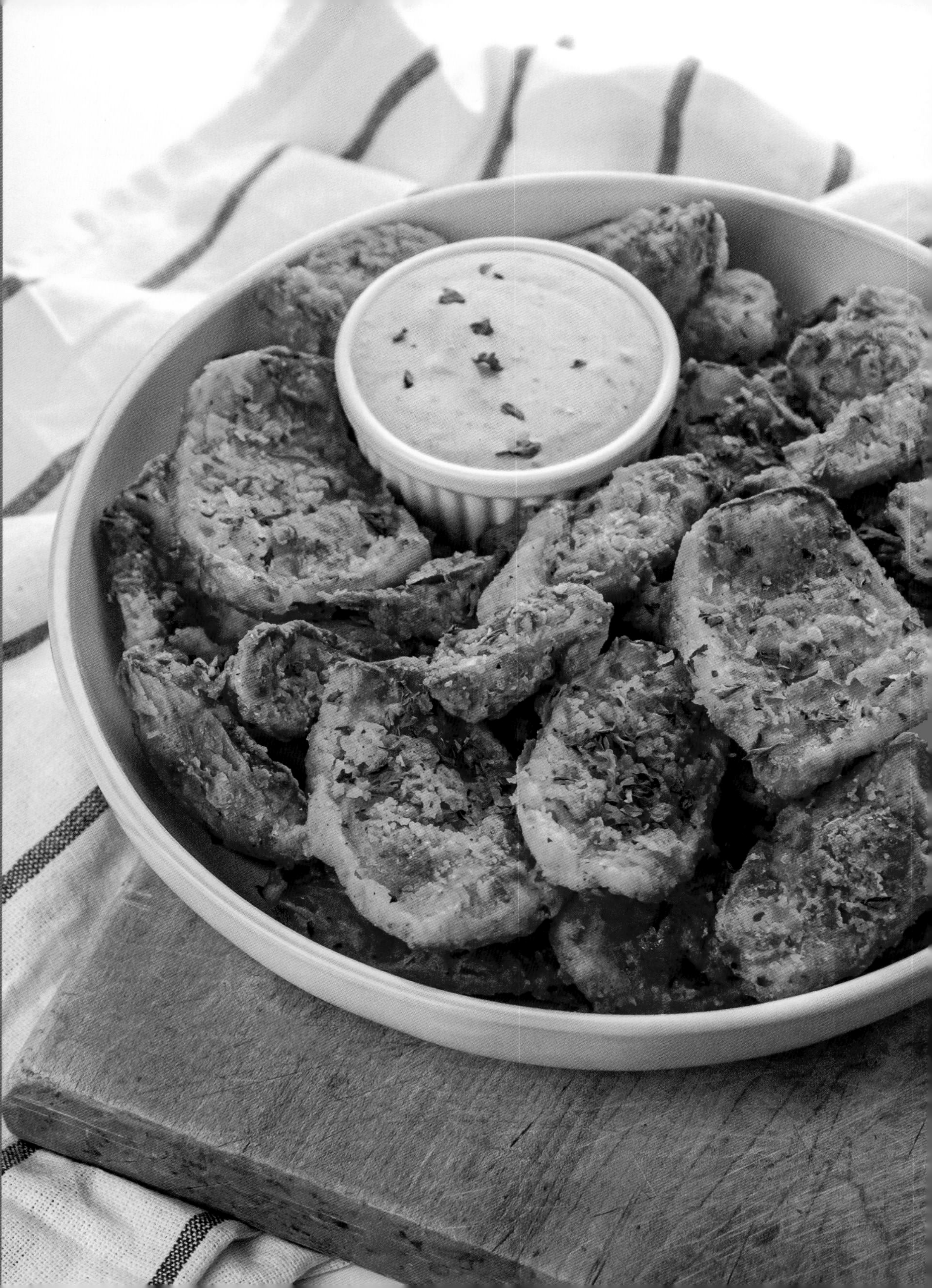

BLOOMING ONION PETALS

Blooming onions quickly became a must-try in the air fryer and for good reason! This restaurant appetizer is loved by many but can be incredibly greasy! Many noted it was hard to get them to turn out like the restaurants, not to mention very messy to make in the air fryer. So I cut the onion into petals, ensuring complete coating coverage, less mess, and way easier to eat (and cook)!

COOK TIME: 25 MIN | EFFORT: EASY

SAUCE

- 3 tablespoons (44 ml) mayo
- 3 tablespoons (44 ml) ketchup
- ¼ teaspoon Worcestershire sauce
- ½ teaspoon horseradish
- ⅛ teaspoon paprika
- ⅛ teaspoon garlic powder
- ⅛ teaspoon onion powder
- ⅛ teaspoon dried oregano
- ¼ teaspoon salt
- ⅛ teaspoon pepper

INGREDIENTS

- 1 large onion
- 1 egg
- 1 tablespoon (15 ml) milk
- 1 cup (130 g) flour
- 1 teaspoon salt
- ½ teaspoon pepper
- ¼ teaspoon cayenne pepper
- ½ teaspoon paprika
- ½ teaspoon garlic powder
- ½ teaspoon onion powder
- ½ teaspoon baking powder
- Oil spray

DIRECTIONS

1. In a small bowl, stir together the mayo, ketchup, Worcestershire sauce, horseradish, paprika, garlic powder, onion powder, oregano, salt, and pepper. Cover and refrigerate.

2. Preheat the air fryer to 350° F (170° C). Cut the onion in half, leaving the root end intact. Cut each half into three wedges, then cut the root ends off. Separate each wedge into petals and set aside.

3. In a small bowl, beat together the egg and milk. In a large resealable bag, combine the flour, salt, pepper, cayenne, paprika, garlic powder, onion powder, and baking powder. Add the onions to the bag, seal, and shake to coat. Shake off the excess flour and transfer the petals to the egg mixture. Shake off the excess egg, and return to the flour mixture, shaking to coat.

4. Spray the air fryer with oil, add the onions, and spray with oil. Cook for 4-8 minutes, flip the petals, spray with oil again, and cook for another 4-8 minutes. Finally, flip the onions once more and cook for 4-8 additional minutes. Serve with the sauce.

MAPLE BACON BRUSSELS SPROUTS

After recently trying Brussels sprouts tossed in bacon and maple syrup, I thought to myself, "I have to try this in the air fryer!" Instead of fresh bacon, where you'd have three-quarters of a package unused, I tried it using bacon bits. Warming the bacon in the maple syrup really infuses the flavor throughout and was a total hit!

COOK TIME: 10 MIN | EFFORT: EASY

INGREDIENTS

- 8 ounces (227 g) Brussels sprouts, halved
- ½ cup (157 ml) pure maple syrup
- 2 tablespoons (25 g) bacon bits
  Oil spray

DIRECTIONS

1. Preheat the air fryer to 350° F (170° C). Add the Brussels sprouts to the air fryer and cook for 6-10 minutes, stirring halfway through.

2. Meanwhile, in a medium saucepan over medium heat, bring the maple syrup and bacon to a simmer. Cook for 5-8 minutes, or until reduced by half. Add the Brussels sprouts to the sauce, stir to coat, and serve.

CRISPY POTATO WEDGES

The air fryer makes some amazing recreations of your favorite fried foods but in a lot healthier way! Never has that been more evident than with these crispy potato wedges; they're perfectly seasoned and ready to be served with an amazing entree!

COOK TIME: 30 MIN | EFFORT: EASY

INGREDIENTS

- 2 medium potatoes, sliced into wedges
- 1 teaspoon salt
- ½ teaspoon pepper
- 1 teaspoon garlic powder
- 1 teaspoon onion powder
- 1 teaspoon paprika
- 2 tablespoons (17 g) cornstarch
  Oil spray

DIRECTIONS

1. In a large bowl, soak the potatoes in cold water for 15 minutes. Remove from the water and pat dry.

2. Preheat the air fryer to 400° F (200° C). In a small bowl, combine the salt, pepper, garlic powder, onion powder, paprika, and cornstarch. In a large bowl, add the potatoes, pour the seasoning mixture over the potatoes, and toss to coat.

3. Spray the air fryer with oil, add the potatoes, spray with oil, and cook for 30 minutes, flipping halfway through, and spraying with more oil. Serve alongside a main dish for a complete meal.

ZUCCHINI AND YELLOW SQUASH AU GRATIN

You've heard of potato au gratin but have you heard of it with zucchini and squash? It totally works and has more nutrients than potatoes! What's not to love about that? Whether squash is your thing or not, give it a try, I'm sure you're going to love it!

COOK TIME: 40 MIN | EFFORT: EASY

INGREDIENTS

- 1 small zucchini, sliced
- 1 small yellow squash, sliced
- 1 tablespoon (14 g) butter
- 3 teaspoons (8 g) flour
- ¾ cup (187 ml) milk
- ½ teaspoon salt
- ¼ teaspoon pepper
- ¼ teaspoon onion powder
- ¼ teaspoon garlic powder
- ¼ cup (27 g) panko breadcrumbs
- 2 tablespoons (12 g) grated Parmesan cheese
- Oil spray

DIRECTIONS

1. Preheat the air fryer to 400° F (200° C). Add the zucchini and squash to the air fryer, spraying lightly with oil, and cook for 13-17 minutes, stirring twice while cooking.

2. Meanwhile, in a small saucepan over medium heat, melt the butter. Whisk in the flour, stirring continuously for 2 minutes. Gradually add in the milk, stirring after each addition. Add in the salt, pepper, onion powder, and garlic powder, stirring until combined.

3. In a small bowl, combine the panko and Parmesan.

4. In a 6-inch baking dish, arrange the zucchini and squash, pour in the sauce, and top with the panko mixture. Reduce the air fryer temperature to 360° F (180° C). Cover the dish with foil and bake for 13-17 minutes. Remove the foil and cook for 3-5 minutes more until golden and bubbly.

ROASTED BROCCOLI WITH ITALIAN HERB BREADCRUMBS

I love broccoli and eat it all the time. This is why I like to change it up now and then just to keep it exciting. That's where this dish came from! Tossed with panko, Italian seasoning, and Parmesan cheese turns simple broccoli into an extraordinary side dish!

COOK TIME: 14 MIN | EFFORT: EASY

INGREDIENTS

- ½ cup (57 g) panko breadcrumbs
- ½ teaspoon Italian seasoning
- 2 tablespoons (12 g) grated Parmesan cheese
- ¼ teaspoon onion powder
- ¼ teaspoon garlic powder
- ½ teaspoon salt
- ¼ teaspoon pepper
- 1 large broccoli head, cut into florets
- 1 tablespoon (15 ml) canola oil
- Oil spray

DIRECTIONS

1. Preheat the air fryer to 400° F (200° C).

2. In a small bowl stir together the panko, Italian seasoning, Parmesan, onion powder, garlic powder, salt, and pepper. In a large bowl, toss the broccoli with oil, add the panko mixture, and toss to coat. Spray the air fryer with oil, add the broccoli, and cook for 10-14 minutes, stirring halfway through to ensure even browning.

3. Serve as an appetizer or alongside a main dish for a complete meal.

THE SWEET
SPOT

If I'm honest, desserts are some of my favorite things to make in the air fryer. When you can make things like donuts, skillet cookies, cheesecake eggrolls, and bread puddings, what's not to love about that?! And that doesn't even scratch the surface. When you've made dinner and the sweet tooth is calling, make sure you bookmark this page to know where this chapter starts!

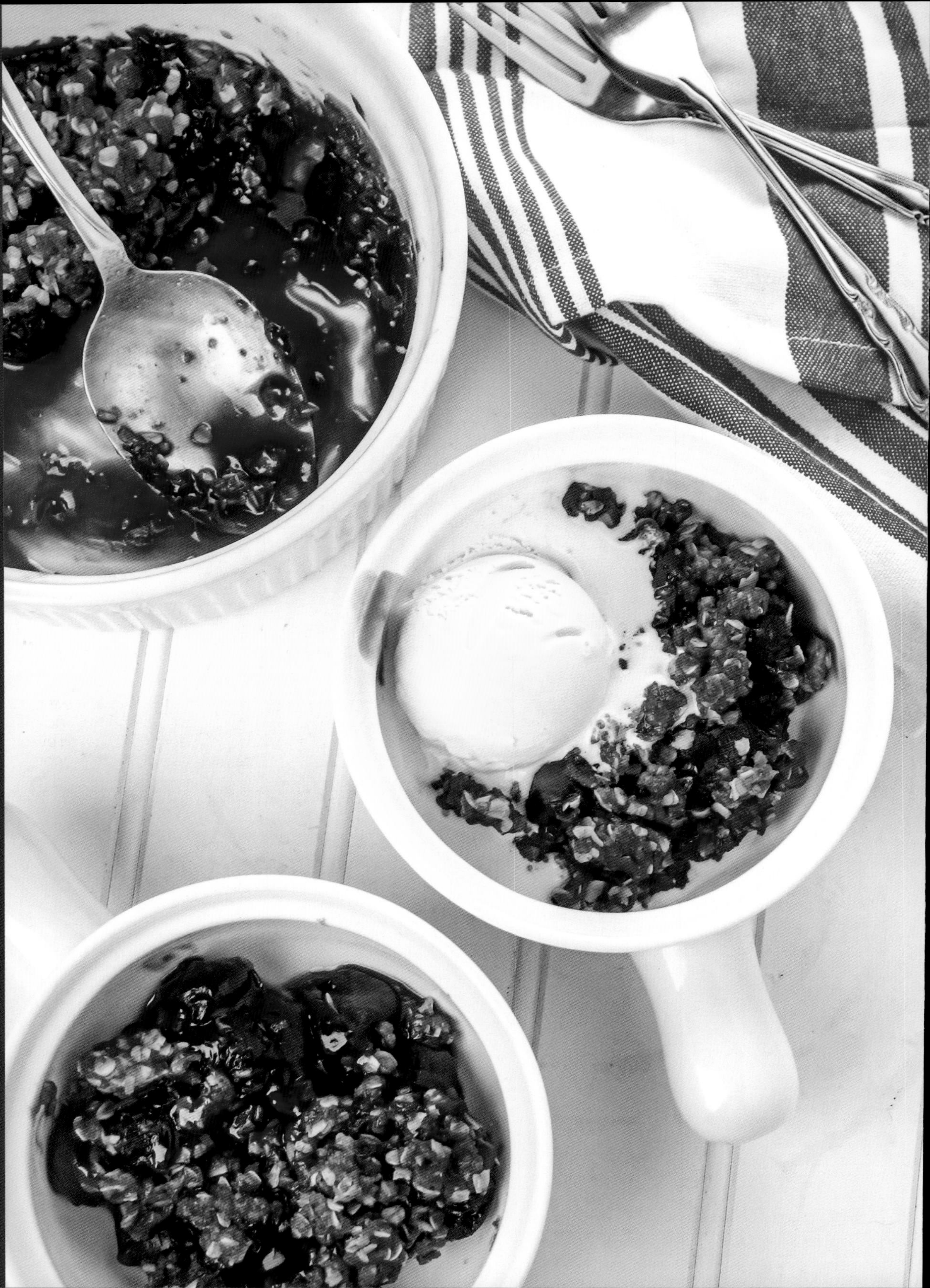

DARK CHERRY OATMEAL CRISP

In the mood for an easy dessert? Look no further! This cherry crisp is sprinkled with an oatmeal topping that turns into a deliciously crispy and cookie-like layer. There's nothing quite like the textural contrasts of this baked dessert!

COOK TIME: 36 MIN | EFFORT: EASY

INGREDIENTS

- 1 (10-ounce or 283 g) bag frozen dark cherries
- ¼ cup (50 g) sugar
- 1½ tablespoons (11 g) cornstarch
- 3 tablespoons (42 g) butter, melted
- 2 tablespoons (25 g) brown sugar
- 3 tablespoons (23 g) flour
- 3 tablespoons (15 g) rolled oats
- ⅛ teaspoon cinnamon

DIRECTIONS

1. In a medium bowl, combine the cherries, sugar, and cornstarch until the cherries are well coated. Pour the cherry mixture into a 6-inch baking dish.

2. Preheat the air fryer to 320° F (160° C). In a small bowl, stir together the butter, brown sugar, flour, oats, and cinnamon until combined. Using your fingers, sprinkle the mixture over the cherries.

3. Cover the baking dish with aluminum foil and place it in the air fryer, cooking for 18-22 minutes. Remove the foil and cook for 10-14 minutes more, until bubbling and the top is browned. Cool for 10 minutes before serving as is, or with a scoop of vanilla ice cream.

CINNAMON STREUSEL PIZZA

If you're looking at this title asking yourself, 'what is a cinnamon streusel pizza?', then let me tell you! It's a homemade dough, topped with cinnamon sugar, oatmeal streusel, and simple icing. This is a dessert you didn't know you needed, until now.

COOK TIME: 12 MIN | EFFORT: EASY

INGREDIENTS

- 6 tablespoons (90 ml) warm water
- 2 teaspoons (8 g) sugar
- ½ packet active dry yeast or 1⅛ teaspoons (3 g)
- 1 tablespoon (15 ml) canola oil
- ½ teaspoon salt
- 1 cup (130 g) flour
- 2 tablespoons (16 g) powdered sugar
- ⅛ teaspoon water

CINNAMON SUGAR

- 1 tablespoon (4 g) sugar
- ¼ teaspoon cinnamon

STREUSEL

- 3 tablespoons (42 g) butter, melted
- 2 tablespoons (27 g) brown sugar
- 3 tablespoons (23 g) flour
- 3 tablespoons (15 g) rolled oats
- ⅛ teaspoon cinnamon

DIRECTIONS

1. In a medium bowl, combine the warm water, sugar, and yeast. Allow the mixture to sit for 5 minutes, once foamy and fragrant, add the oil, salt, and flour. Stir the mixture until a dough forms. Transfer the dough to a clean, greased bowl. Cover with plastic wrap and allow to rise for 1 hour or until doubled in size.

2. Preheat the air fryer to 350º F (170º C). In a small bowl, combine the sugar and cinnamon. In a second small bowl, stir together the butter, brown sugar, flour, oats, and cinnamon.

3. Spray a 6-inch baking pan with oil and press the dough into the pan. Sprinkle with the cinnamon-sugar mixture, and sprinkle the streusel on top. Cook for 8-12 minutes.

4. Meanwhile, in a small bowl, stir together the powdered sugar and water. The icing should be thin but not watery. Drizzle over the cinnamon pizza, cut, and serve for a delicious cinnamon dessert.

RASPBERRY CHEESECAKE EGGROLLS

If you haven't noticed, I love finger food because it is such a fun way to eat. What could be more fun than stuffing eggrolls with cheesecake?! Crispy eggroll wrappers filled with ingredients for a raspberry cheesecake make this dessert as delicious as they are entertaining!

COOK TIME: 10 MIN | EFFORT: EASY

INGREDIENTS

- ½ cup (116 g) cream cheese, softened
- ¼ cup (33 g) powdered sugar
- ½ teaspoon vanilla extract
- 1 graham cracker, crumbled
- 2 tablespoons (40 g) raspberry preserves, plus more for serving.
- 4 eggroll wrappers
- Oil spray

DIRECTIONS

1. In a small bowl, combine the cream cheese, powdered sugar, and vanilla.

2. On a work surface, lay a eggroll wrapper down in a diamond shape. Scoop 2 tablespoons of the cream cheese mixture, ¼ of the graham cracker, and ½ tablespoon of the preserves into the middle of the wrapper. Fold in the bottom, left, and right corners, gently pressing to remove any air bubbles. Using your finger, brush the top corner with water, and roll up to seal. Place it seam side down and repeat with the remaining eggrolls.

3. Preheat the air fryer to 320° F (160° C). Spray the air fryer with oil, add the eggrolls, spray with oil, and cook for 6-10 minutes, flipping halfway through.

4. Meanwhile, in a small bowl, scoop more raspberry preserves and microwave for 30-45 seconds until saucy. Serve the eggrolls with the raspberry sauce for dipping.

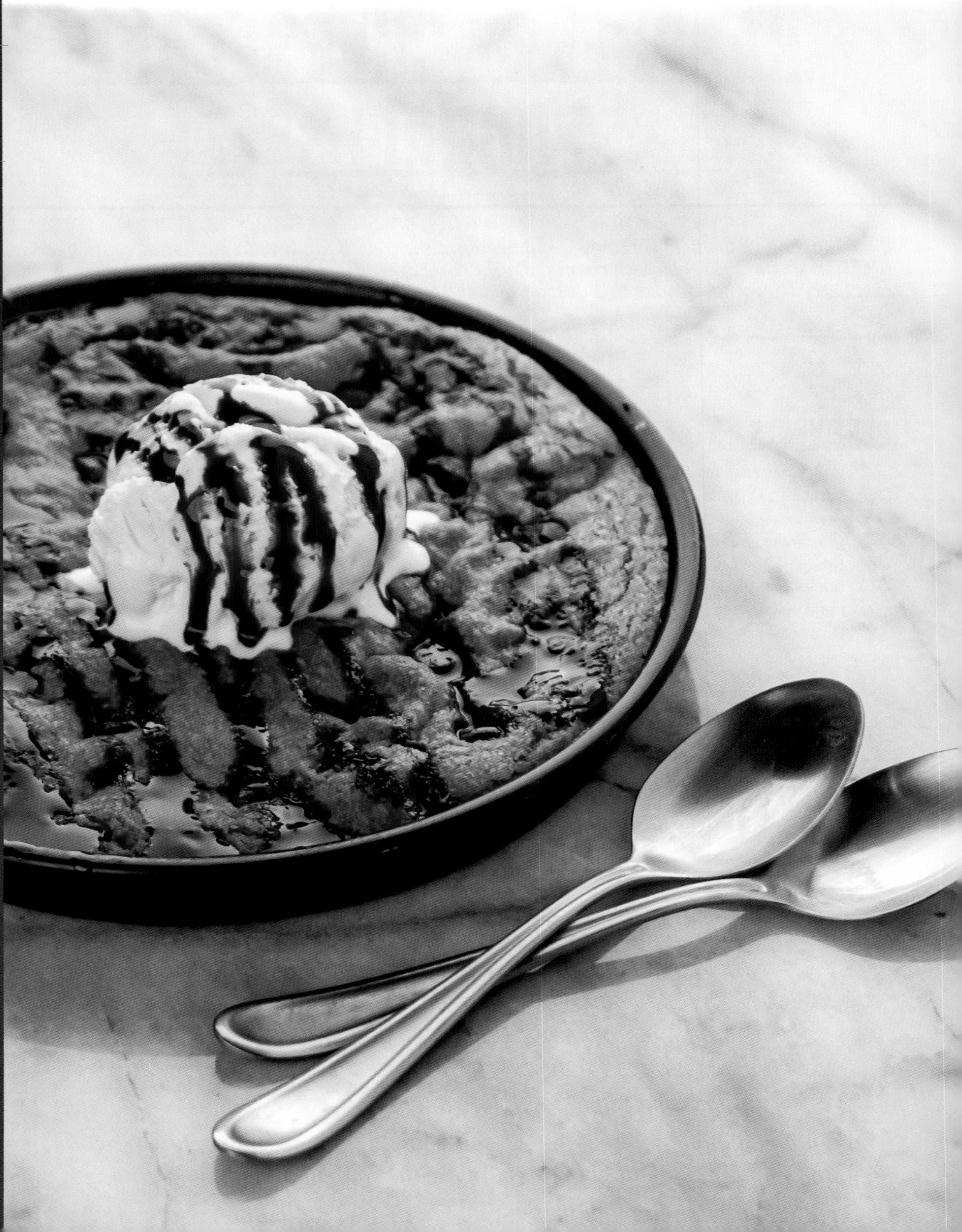

CHOCOLATE CHIP SKILLET COOKIE

Chocolate chip cookies are one of my favorite cookies, but making a whole batch for just two people isn't the best thing for my waistline. So I have made this simple skillet cookie that is perfect for two!

COOK TIME: 14 MIN | EFFORT: EASY

INGREDIENTS

- 6 tablespoons (84 g) butter, room temperature
- ¼ cup (50 g) brown sugar
- 3 tablespoons (36 g) sugar
- 1 egg yolk
- ½ teaspoon vanilla extract
- ⅔ cup (80 g) flour
- ¼ teaspoon baking soda
- ¼ cup (43 g) chocolate chips
- Vanilla ice cream, optional
- Chocolate syrup, optional

DIRECTIONS

1. Preheat the air fryer to 340° F (170° C). In a medium bowl, stir together the butter, brown sugar, and sugar. Add the egg yolk and vanilla, until combined.

2. In a separate medium bowl, whisk together the flour and baking soda. Pour the flour mixture into the butter mixture, stirring until fully combined, then fold in the chocolate chips.

3. Spoon the mixture into a 6-inch baking pan, place in the air fryer, and cook for 10-14 minutes, until golden brown. Serve as is or topped with vanilla ice cream and chocolate syrup.

BREAD PUDDING WITH PRALINE SAUCE

Bread pudding is a fantastic way to use up leftover bread and can make for a great dessert! This one is easy and made even easier when made in the air fryer. Topped with a delicious, homemade praline sauce, you may find yourself even saving bread to have for it.

COOK TIME: 45 MIN | EFFORT: EASY

INGREDIENTS

- 2 cups (120 ml) milk
- 3 eggs, beaten
- ¾ cup (150 g) sugar
- 1 teaspoon ground cinnamon
- 1 teaspoon vanilla extract
- 6 slices day-old brioche bread

SAUCE

- ½ cup (100 g) brown sugar
- ½ cup (112 g) butter

DIRECTIONS

1. Preheat the air fryer to 350° F (170° C). Spray a 6-inch baking dish with oil.

2. In a medium bowl, stir together the milk, eggs, sugar, cinnamon, and vanilla until fully combined.

3. Add the bread to the baking dish. Pour the milk mixture over the top, then gently press to ensure that the bread is soaked. Set aside for 10 minutes.

4. Cover the baking dish with foil and place it in the air fryer, cooking for 28-32 minutes. Remove the foil and cook for 8-12 more minutes. Let sit for 10 minutes before serving.

5. Meanwhile, in a small pan over medium heat, combine the butter and brown sugar. Bring the mixture to a boil, reduce the heat to low, stirring occasionally for 3-5 minutes, until the sugar is completely dissolved.

6. Serve the bread pudding with the praline sauce and enjoy!

APPLE CINNAMON HAND PIES

Sometimes good things come in small packages, and apple pie doesn't have to be different! Everything you love about a warm apple pie in the palm of your hand. While delicious on its own, it can only be made better when served with a little vanilla ice cream.

COOK TIME: 22 MIN | EFFORT: EASY

FILLING

- 1 medium granny smith apple, peeled and diced
- 2 teaspoons (8 g) sugar
- 2 teaspoons (8 g) brown sugar
- ¼ teaspoon ground cinnamon
- ¼ teaspoon vanilla extract
- ¼ cup (59 ml) water

INGREDIENTS

- ½ cup (65 g) flour
- 3 tablespoons (42 g) butter
- 2 tablespoons (30 ml) ice-cold water
- 1 teaspoon sugar
- 1 tablespoon (15 ml) milk
  Sanding sugar, optional
  Vanilla ice cream, optional for serving

DIRECTIONS

1. In a small saucepan over medium heat, add the apples, sugar, brown sugar, cinnamon, vanilla, and water. Bring the mixture to a simmer, cover, and reduce heat to medium-low. Cook for 10 minutes, or until most of the water is absorbed and the apples are tender. Allow to cool to room temperature.

2. In a small bowl, using your fingers, combine the flour and butter until the mixture resembles coarse crumbs. Gradually, add the water, while stirring with a fork, until a dough forms. Divide the dough into two even-sized balls.

3. Preheat the air fryer to 400° F (200° C). On a lightly floured work surface, roll each of the dough balls out into an 9-inch circle. Fill each circle with half of the apple filling, fold over, and crimp the edges with a fork to seal, and cut three vents on top.

4. Carefully line the air fryer with parchment paper and add the hand pies, cooking for 8-12 minutes. Allow to cool for 5 minutes before serving.

COOKIE BUTTER PUDDING CAKE

Much like a molten lava cake, this gooey self-saucing cake is made with speculoos cookie butter (you know, the airline cookie), so you know it's going to be amazing! The best part? It's only three ingredients! Topped with ice cream, this may just be the ultimate dessert for two.

COOK TIME: 32 MIN | EFFORT: EASY

INGREDIENTS

- 1¼ cups (300 g) cookie butter spread, divided
- 2 eggs, separated
- ¼ cup (60 ml) milk

DIRECTIONS

1. Preheat the air fryer to 320° F (160° C). Spoon ½ cup of the cookie butter into a 6-inch baking dish and spread evenly over the base of the dish. Set aside.

2. In a large bowl, using a hand mixer, beat the remaining cookie butter with the egg yolks and milk until combined.

3. In a separate bowl using a hand mixer with clean beaters, beat the egg whites to stiff peaks. Fold half of the egg whites into the cookie butter mixture, until just combined, then fold in the remaining whites until no streaks remain.

4. Gently pour the batter into the baking dish and spread in an even layer on top of the cookie butter. Bake for 28-32 minutes, until the a toothpick inserted to the center comes out clean. Cool for 5 minutes before serving.

CARAMELIZED BANANAS WITH WHIPPED MARSCARPONE

Need ideas to use up extra bananas? Then this recipe is for you! Sprinkled with brown sugar that turns into a crunchy caramelized topping and served with whipped mascarpone cheese, a delicious dessert is just minutes away. It doesn't get much better than this!

COOK TIME: 10 MIN | EFFORT: EASY

INGREDIENTS

- 2 large ripe bananas, peeled and sliced lengthwise
- 1 teaspoon lemon juice
- ¼ cup (16 g) brown sugar, divided
- ⅓ cup (75 g) mascarpone cheese
- 2 tablespoons (30 ml) pure maple syrup
- ¼ teaspoon ground cinnamon

DIRECTIONS

1. Preheat the air fryer to 400° F (200° C). Drizzle the bananas with lemon juice and top with 1 tablespoon of brown sugar per banana slice.

2. Lay parchment paper in the basket of the air fryer. Place the bananas, cut sides up, on a wire rack, and carefully place it into the basket. Cook until the sugar has melted and browned, about 7 minutes.

3. Meanwhile, in a small bowl, stir the mascarpone until softened, then add in the maple syrup and cinnamon, stirring until thoroughly combined. Serve with caramelized bananas.

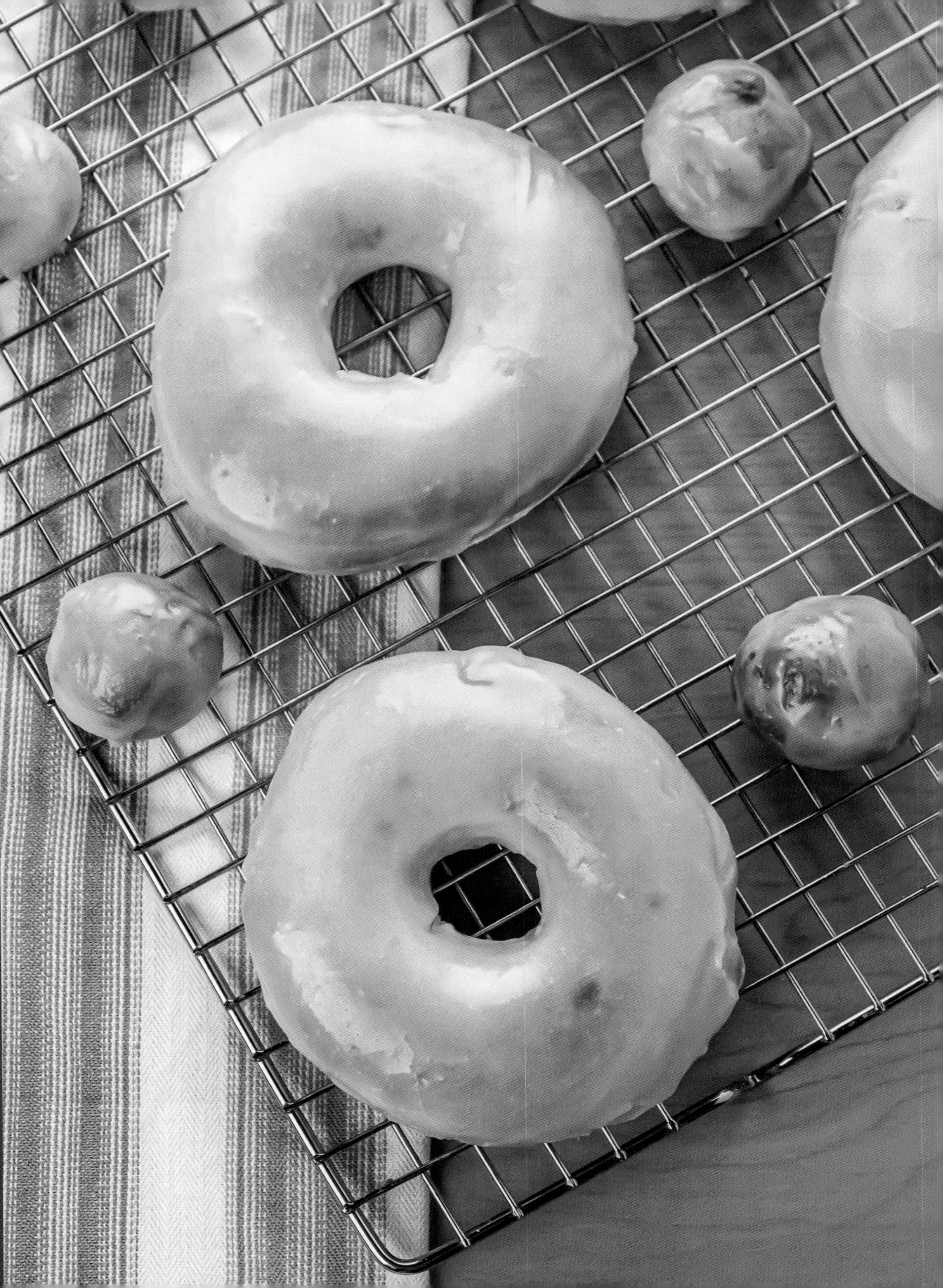

CLASSIC GLAZED DONUTS

While more commonly eaten as a breakfast item, we all know donuts are essentially a dessert. So why not serve them as such?! These fluffy and airy donuts are the 'healthier' alternative to frying but with all the flavor and only half of the guilt.

COOK TIME: 10 MIN | EFFORT: MODERATE

INGREDIENTS

- ½ cup (118 ml) milk, warm
- 2 tablespoons (24 g) sugar
- 1 teaspoon active dry yeast
- ¼ teaspoon salt
- 1 egg
- 2 tablespoons (28 g) butter, melted
- 1¾ cups (224 g) flour, plus more if needed

GLAZE

- 3 tablespoons (42 g) butter
- 1 cup (130 g) powdered sugar
- ½ teaspoon vanilla extract
- 2 tablespoons (30 ml) hot water

DIRECTIONS

1. In a stand mixer, add the milk, sugar, and yeast, letting sit for 5 minutes until foamy. Add the salt, egg, butter, and flour, mixing on low speed until the dough no longer sticks to the bowl, adding more flour, 1 tablespoon at a time, if needed. Increase the speed to medium and knead for 5 minutes, until the dough is elastic and smooth.

2. In a large greased bowl, add the dough, cover with plastic wrap, and let rise for 1 hour in a warm place, until doubled in size.

3. On a floured surface, roll out the dough to about ½-inch thick. Using a 3-inch round cutter, cut out 4 donuts and a 1-inch round cutter to remove the center. Place the donuts and holes on a lightly floured baking sheet, spray lightly with oil, and let rise for 45 minutes in a warm place, until doubled in size.

4. Preheat the air fryer to 350° F (170° C). Spray the air fryer with oil, add the donuts, and spray with oil, cook for 3-5 minutes, until golden brown. Repeat with the remaining donuts.

5. Meanwhile, in a small saucepan over medium heat, melt the butter. Stir in the powdered sugar and vanilla until smooth. Remove from the heat and stir in the hot water, 1 tablespoon at a time, until the icing is thin, but not watery, adding more if necessary.

6. Dip the hot donuts and holes into the glaze. Place on a wire rack set over a rimmed baking sheet for the excess glaze to drip off. Let sit until the glaze hardens, about 10 minutes.

ABOUT THE AUTHOR

Hi, I'm Drew! And before you ask, yes, I am writing my 'about the author.' No, I won't be using the third person because it feels incredibly awkward. So, who am I, and when did I start writing cookbooks? Well, I started baking at a very young age, my grandma would pick me up and plop me on the counter right next to the mixer, and I would "help" her measure ingredients. Looking back, I realize I wasn't helping her at all, but she allowed me to be involved, and little did we know where that would eventually lead.

I never stopped baking but eventually found myself doing a lot more cooking, and in 2012 I started a cooking blog to share recipes I was creating; this site is now called BestRecipes.co. That eventually turned into a recipe magazine that I served as the editor in chief. That magazine connected me to the publishing world, and that's when I started writing cookbooks, which pretty much catches you up! But beyond cookbooks, I've had my recipes featured in several magazines; how cool is that?! I'm still feeling the excitement!

Now I haven't mentioned this yet, but I am a self-taught cook, never went to culinary school, and that used to make me a little insecure. It wasn't until later that I realized this might be to my advantage. I write recipes for everyday home cooks, like you, and I'm sure going to culinary school would have been a fantastic experience, it would've also complicated my process. How so? Well, chefs can dice an onion, perfectly uniform, in like 5 seconds flat. I can't do that, and I'll guess you can't either! But if I could, can you imagine how much more complicated my recipes would be? I know getting an onion chopped in a few minutes is a win, and that's what normal is. That's what keeps my cooking simple and approachable for everyone! And that has always been and will always be my goal.

If you've read this far, thank you! Truly, it has been an honor and a dream come true to be able to write recipes for you. I hope you have enjoyed this book and will check out my website and other cookbooks!

ACKNOWLEDGMENTS

Thank you to all of my friends and family, you have been such a huge support in the production of this book. The honest feedback and willingness to help me is truly what made this book possible!

A special thank you to my Facebook group, Just Air Fryer Recipes, who gave me ideas and feedback through every phase of this book.

Lastly, I want to thank you, the readers, without you, I would not be able to do what I love to do

JOIN OUR FACEBOOK GROUP!
https://bestrecipes.co/afgroup

ABOUT THE PUBLISHER

We were founded in 2012 with a mission, making meals simple but always delicious! We use everyday supermarket ingredients and easy-to-follow steps so you can spend minutes (not hours) getting dinner on the table. Our team loves food, and we believe dinner should be fun and easy — and should never feel like a chore. Comprised of chefs and home cooks like you, who believe all recipes need to be approachable for everyone, not just the pros. Foods from all across the globe help to inspire us, so we take those often complex dishes, and break them down — making them as simple as they can be. That means no matter what your cooking skill level is, you'll be able to make the recipe perfect every time! Because we all know, life can be complicated, but cooking certainly doesn't have to be. Simple meals get on the table faster, and food brings people together! At the end of the day, that's what it's all about — bringing people together, one meal at a time. We think of you, our reader, as we develop each and every recipe. Because if these recipes don't serve you, they're serving no one.

INDEX

INDEX

INDEX

INDEX

INDEX